Tales of Knock Your Socks Off Service

Permissions

The American Red Cross: Paragon of Grace Under Fire
Excerpted from http://www.redcross.org. © copyright 1997, The American National Red Cross. All rights reserved.

Chicken Soup for the Soul at Work: 101 Stories of Courage, Compassion & Creativity in the Workplace, Jack Canfield and Mark Victor Hansen. Health Communications Inc., 1996.
Fly in Your Soup? How about a Latex Glove in your Stir Fry? © Richard Porter. Reprinted with permission. All rights reserved.
Customer Service is not a Mickey Mouse Affair. © Valerie Oberle, Disney University. Reprinted with permission. All rights reserved.
Jessie's Glove. © Richard Porter. Reprinted with permission. All rights reserved.

Customers as Partners: Building Relationships that Last, Chip R. Bell, Berrett-Koehler Publishers, 1994. © Chip R. Bell. Reprinted with permission. All rights reserved.
A Really Private Proposal

Fabled Service: Ordinary Acts, Extraordinary Outcomes, Betsy Sanders, Pfeiffer & Co., © 1995 by Pfeiffer, an imprint of Jossey-Bass Inc., Publishers. Reprinted with permission. All rights reserved.
The Gospel According to Nordstrom

Reader's Digest
Officers of the Law Need Kind Words, Too
"Good Morning, Bonanza!" submitted by Susan Haight, 9/96
Going through puberty in the waiting room, contributed by Carole J. Hart, 11/94
V-I-S-A, contributed by Cathy Mosely, 10/96
Customer under charged for ham, contributed by Carol Taler, 10/96

The Real Heros of Business . . . and Not a CEO Among Them, by Bill Fromm and Len Schlesinger. Copyright © 1994 by Bill Fromm and Len Schlesinger. Used by permission of Doubleday, a division of Bantam Doubleday Dell Publishing Group, Inc.
Alan Wilk: A Passion for Clogged Drains

The Service Edge: 101 Companies that Profit from Customer Care, Ron E. Zemke, New American Library Publishing, 1989. © Ron Zemke. Reprinted with permission. All rights reserved
Delta People Love to Fly—and this One Loves to Serve; Playing by Stew's Rules; Good Enough? Let it Slide? Not in Ed Lennon's World; No Money=No Service? Not in Southern Bell Rep's World.

The Service Edge Newsletter, **Lakewood Publications, Minneapolis, MN.**
Beyond "Shirt Off Your Back" Service; Two Weeks Before Store Opening, Neiman Marcus Makes Time For Service; Nordstrom Strikes Again; Service with a Smell; Going where Few Have Gone Before; L. L. Bean Again; George Jetson—And Wendy's—to the Rescue; Dogged Pursuit of Customer Satisfaction Wins National Car Rental for Eternity; Just the Fax, Ma'am; Victimized by a Paper Landslide; If at First You Don't Succeed, Recover, Recover—and then Recover Again; A Premature Reservation—and a Mind Blowing Redemption; Taking a Chicken Lickin, and Still Tickin; Retail Redress; His Name was Freddie; Into Harm's Way: 3 Tales of Hurricane Heroics; Never, Never, Never Quit.

Wall Street Journal, *"Penny Nirider has an Unusual View: She Likes her Customers,"* by Thomas Petzinger, Jr., Reprinted by permission of the Wall Street Journal, © 1996 Dow Jones and Company, Inc. All rights reserved worldwide.

Wal-Mart Cares About Kids
Sharon Webber, Wal-Mart Stores, Inc., Bensonville, AR.
Http://www.wal-mart.com excerpted with permission. All rights reserved.

Tales of Knock Your Socks Off Service

Service

Inspiring Stories of Outstanding Customer Service

by Kristin Anderson and Ron Zemke

amacom

American Management Association

New York • Atlanta • Boston • Chicago • Kansas City • San Francisco • Washington, D.C.
Brussels • Mexico City • Tokyo • Toronto

This book is available at a special
discount when ordered in bulk quantities.
For information, contact Special Sales Department,
AMACOM, a division of American Management Association,
1601 Broadway, New York, NY 10019.

This publication is designed to provide accurate and authoritative information in re-
gard to the subject matter covered. It is sold with the understanding that the publisher
is not engaged in rendering legal, accounting, or other professional service. If legal advice or other expert assistance is reauired, the services of a competent professional person should be sought.

Library of Congress Cataloging-in-Publication Data

Anderson, Kristin.
    Tales of knock your socks off service : inspiring stories of outstanding customer
service / Kristin Anderson, Ron Zemke.
        p.   cm.
    ISBN 0-8144-7971-5
    1. Customer services—United States—Case studies.   2. Consumer
satisfaction—United States—Case studies.   I. Zemke, Ron.   II. Title.
HF5415.5.A535   1997
658.8'12—dc21   97-29375
                                                                          CIP

KNOCK YOUR SOCKS OFF SERVICE®
is a registered trademark of Performance Research Associates, Inc.

Printing number

10   9   8   7   6   5   4   3   2   1

Table of Contents

3 Savoring Those "Daily Delights" 48

4 Service From the Heart   73

5 At Risk of Life and Limb   103

6 Memorable People 126

7 Keeping Great Company 147

8 Tales from the Service Zone 172

Acknowledgments

There are many, many people to thank for helping us bring this book into being. First and foremost are the people who contributed stories to this book. Each is acknowledged as their wonderful stories of brilliant service are told. We need particularly to thank Mary Ann Jeffery of Cadillac, Beverly Holmes and Dick Mensch of Lands' End, Nicole Jacobsen of the Colorado Rockies, Gail Wasserman of American Express, Jill Packey of Norwest Corp., Carol Olander of H.E. Butt, Darlene Faquin of Federal Express, John Quinley of the National Park Service, Rick Harmon of the American Water Works Association, Kristen Petrella of UPS, Tracy Hollingsworth of Jones Intercable, Allen Stasiewski of St. Luke's Hospital, Katrina Etter of Professional Travel Corporation, and Beth Adair of Beverly Enterprises for giving us access to so many wonderful service stories from the annals of their organizations.

Very, very special "thank yous" go to Hank Kennedy, Steve Arkin, Irene Majuk, and our editor Ellen Kadin, of AMACOM. Each influenced this book in a special way and has been very, very helpful to its final form and substance, as have our partners Chip Bell and Tom Connellan, who scouted out many of the best stories. A special gold star goes out to Susan Zemke, who once again proved she has excellent taste in tales short and tall.

An equally special commendation goes to John Bush who has illustrated every one of the *Knock Your Socks Off Service* books. John brings his rare talent and special eye to every project and makes us glad he enjoys the world of customer care as much as we do.

Two more people on the home team need recognition for their absolutely, positively irreplaceable work; Dave Zielinski and Jill Applegate. Dave is the Godfather of this book, and Jill its Godmother. They wrote, edited, and sweat right alongside us, and on top of that, they were 100% in charge of communicating with the contributors, clarifying stories we didn't quite understand, and getting feedback on the tweaking and fussing we did with other people's prose... and they definitely kept us from misrepresenting or misinterpreting the contributors. There simply would be no book without them. Both deserve hugs, kisses, and long longevous furloughs.

To each and every one of these people we can but say "Thanks Guys! You are the best. You are the embodiment of great service!"

Ron Zemke
Kristin Anderson
August 1997

Preface

This Book: It's About You

Working with people—serving customers—can be a rewarding, fulfilling and uplifting way to make a living or spend a life. Working with people—serving customers—can also be among the most frustrating, infuriating, draining, fatiguing, and thankless jobs imaginable.

Which one it is for you... depends.

It depends on the organization you work for—and its policies and practices. It depends on the customers you work with—and the challenges and opportunities they present. It depends on the time and the tools you have for doing the job you've been asked to do. And it depends, most of all, on you. How you think, and feel, and care about the challenge of helping people—who are almost always total strangers—solve their problems, find what they need, and have their fears and anxieties calmed and dispelled at your hands.

But you know most of that already. Our guess is you wouldn't be reading this book if you didn't. You wouldn't have lasted long enough to read any book about customer service if those challenges didn't in some way stir and excite your heart, soul, or psyche. Congratulations! You are a winner in a world that sometimes seems overflowing with whiners and an infinite stream of people with problems and grievances and very few smiles. This book is about—and for—you.

This is a very simple book, really. It is an anthology, a collection of stories about the things you—and people like you around the world—do to delight your customers and make the few precious minutes they spend with you positive and memorable. It is a collection of stories that answer the question, "Why can't you get good service anymore?" with a smiling and gentle, "Oh, but you can. You really can."

It is also a testament to the infinite variety and multitude of forms memorable customer service can—and almost always does—take. There are eight lessons to this testament, all told in the words of the customers or co-workers who experienced or witnessed the memorable events of the stories recorded here.

- The first we call stories of "Above and Beyond." Tales of service that go well beyond a customer's expectations and hopes for help, stories of near-heroic acts that ensure customers walk away with smiles on their faces, not disappointment in their eyes.

- Second come stories we call tales of "Great Saves" or spectacular service recovery. Stories of customer service pros who, in some cases, literally move heaven and earth to fix a problem for a customer; often a problem the service person's own company caused.

- Then there are stories we call "Daily Delights," tales of service that is a step above average and that delighted a customer or patron or client—and formed a lasting, positive impression. Often an impression so strong customers took time to tell the tale to others; tales we are pleased to be passing along.

- "Service From the Heart" is about people from all walks of life, serving people because it's a privilege—and because it's the right thing to do, not simply because it's a job. These are tales of people who serve in a way that lifts and ennobles, that shares a little bit of the eternal in themselves.

- "At Risk of Life and Limb" are our tales of people who not only went above and beyond for a customer, but who also often, quite literally, put themselves at some personal risk to ensure a customer's well-being or safety. They are stories of uncompromising actions by people like you or us that make us proud to be in the same business.

- "Memorable People" salutes a parade of individuals who exhibit great ideas or quick smiles or winning ways with such constancy and universality that they have become living-and-breathing benchmarks for great service. They are super role models for us all.

- "Keeping Great Company" is about workers under the same roof who seem to be inspired either by each other, the challenge, the organization that employs them or by some mysterious "X" factor. For these co-workers and companies, "good enough" simply *isn't*, when it comes to serving others.

- "The Service Zone" takes you on a small side trip to a land where Rod Serling would be right at home. The Zone offers tales of customer service strangeness that made us laugh, shake our heads in disbelief or wonder, sigh, and often, giggle. They are tales we couldn't resist sharing with you. Think of them as a verbal tonic, stress-relief medication in print, the hidden prize in the Mardi Gras King's Cake. They're a reward for your good work—the work you and thousands of your colleagues did to make this book possible.

If you enjoy reading this volume half as much as we enjoyed collecting, sorting, editing, and compiling the stories in it into final form, we will have done our jobs well. We hope these stories will inspire, inform, challenge, and amuse you—just as they have inspired, informed, challenged, and amused us.

Above all else, we hope these stories reconfirm for you the feeling and fact that you are, indeed, engaged in one of the finest pursuits possible—serving others. Thank you for that decision and that commitment. Think of this book then, as our "Thank You" to you and your peers who spend your days—and in some cases your nights—spreading great service to others.

About the Stories

The stories in this volume—like all stories—come from many sources. Some are "found" stories; stories we read and loved in other books, newspapers, magazines, newsletters, and in-company publications that we wanted to pass along for your reading pleasure. Some are stories we've stumbled across on our own—memorable service incidents from our lives and the lives of our partners, friends, and co-workers. Several are stories from Lakewood Publication's, *The Service Edge Newsletter*, for which Ron Zemke served as editor from 1988 to1996. We thank Lakewood for allowing us to share these stories with you. The greatest source, however, has been the hundreds of customer service people across the world who've taken the time to write down and send to us the memorable service incidents of their lives—stories of great service they've received and great service they've witnessed colleagues and friends giving and receiving. Our heartfelt thanks to all of you.

We've taken the best of the best of these stories, followed up on them to include as much detail as possible, and presented them here for your contemplation and enjoyment. We have acknowledged all contributions and sources at the end of the book.

By one guesstimate, we've included about fifteen percent of the treasure trove of great service stories we've amassed since we began the "Knock Your Socks Off Service" series in 1991. We hope you approve of our selections—and we hope they inspire you to keep doing the things that made these stories possible.

1

Service "Above and Beyond"

Ever have one of those days when things have gone from bad to worse to unbelievably horrific? When, say, it's raining cats and dogs and there is a leak in the roof and you've lost your car keys and the daycare is closed and the sitter hasn't shown up and you're late for work and there is a staff meeting first thing and one of the kids has a fever and you don't feel all that great yourself? And deep in your heart you're wishing for a beatifically smiling Samaritan to show up with a limousine and an umbrella and a hot cup of coffee and a cinnamon roll, with the words,

1

"Don't worry. Everything will be fine. Just leave it to me," emblazoned on his or her superhero cape?

It's not as if your life or marriage or mental health is at risk, just your day. And when that magic does strike and someone does reach out and give you a little extra help, or takes a little extra time with you—or just acknowledges that you've had one heck of a bad day—it really does help and is more than memorable. Call it:

"Service Above and Beyond"

What follows are tales of customer service people who—for whatever reason—have gone beyond the call of duty for a customer or client. Call them Good Samaritans, Humanitarians, or simply Good People. Or call them a little crazy. Call them what you like, but the people in these 23 stories of "Above and Beyond" service share one simple thing: They have reached out to someone with a problem or quandary they can't quite handle on their own—and they've done something wonderful and creative and ingenious and kind. They have served "Above and Beyond" to the benefit and surprise and admiration of others. And they did it simply because they could, and it seemed the right and only thing to do.

These tales of their "Above and Beyond" deeds are a testament to the energy it's possible to bring to the customer service job—and the return that flows from it.

An Olympian Save

Early in 1996, I had one of those brainstorms that you sometimes come to regret, "Let's all go to the Olympics next year! It'll be a great company outing."

The ticket application process should have warned us away. But it didn't. So 20 hours and 34 pages later of "On Line B list your third choice for Thursday events bearing in mind that its total price cannot exceed the price cost index of the principality of Munwango for the fiscal year of 1907," we affixed seven pounds of postage to our wish list of events and shipped the package off to the 1996 Olympic Games request lottery office. Remember, you couldn't actually buy tickets, only put your name in a drawing for tickets, but you were required to prepay the tickets in the event that your name was actually drawn and you got tickets for the events you wanted. (No, we couldn't exactly follow it either.)

Eight weeks later, we received notice from the Olympic ticket folks informing us that our lottery ticket application had been rejected. The credit limit on our Visa Card, it seems, was less than the maximum amount that might be due if we were actually allowed all the tickets we'd requested, and ... as the ads clearly said, they didn't take American Express. We would have to correct the "error," we were informed, then resubmit our application. Of course, we were no longer eligible for the June lottery, but could qualify for the leftovers lottery.

Since the Visa in question was an extension of a checking account with a pretty deep line of credit, we went screeching down the street to Nan Clarke's office. Nan, our First Bank Minneapolis banker, was taken aback as well. A little phone work disclosed that while we had indeed had a line of credit sufficient for the cost of tickets we were angling for, we would indeed exceed our *daily* charge card limit—if, in the very unlikely event, we indeed drew all the first choice tickets we were requesting. An event as likely as being struck by a meteorite while dancing the Macarena.

Exactly who Nan called at Visa, and who in the bank she drew into the fray, she hasn't—and won't—specify. We can say for sure that three hours later she called to let us know that she was on the case and with a touch of glee in her voice added,

"This one's getting to be fun." Toward the end of the day, Nan was back on the phone to us, "We had a little meeting with some Visa people," she announced, "so we should have something interesting by morning." True to her prescient word, we were greeted the next morning by a fax from the Olympic ticket committee informing us that our application was indeed back in the lottery—with no change in our drawing queue placement, and wishing us good luck with our selections.

That afternoon, Nan was on our door step with an assortment of Olympic shirts, caps, and duffel bags—and a sincere apology. "I'm glad you called," she confided, "we could have had a lot of disappointed customers." She made us feel good about the extra work we'd put her through, and not at all like the `customers from hell' we, at one point, were beginning to feel we'd become.

Oh, and the Olympics. We hit the jackpot there, too. Gymnastics, Diving, Boxing, Track and Field. And the warm, toasty feeling that we have a banker who indeed is on our side and not just a name on an account activity summary. Someone willing to put a little "Above and Beyond" at our service when need be.

Ron Zemke

Barred from Barcelona: TWA Soothes Disheartened Would-Be Travelers

In the spring of 1996, Catherine Schmehling and her husband booked a dream trip from their small town in the Midwest to Barcelona, Spain, through St. Louis-based Trans World Airlines.

But not all went as promised in the travel itinerary. During a flight connection at John F. Kennedy Airport in New York, Catherine tripped and fell, sustaining a nasty black eye and other injuries. Aida Delfaus, a Trans World employee, heard about the accident and went out to see what she could do to help the passenger. Catherine was hurt badly; she could barely walk. Aida called management and the Port Authority Police, who determined that Catherine definitely needed medical assistance, and certainly could not travel on to Spain. Mrs. Schmehling was taken to St. Mary's Hospital.

Aida felt bad for the Schmehlings. Here was an elderly couple quite overwhelmed by JFK airport and the prospect of spending the next few days in New York City. It was their first visit ever to the Big Apple, and under such terribly trying circumstances. Add to that the depression of missing their dream vacation to Spain, and their dismay and confusion is quite understandable. Aida arranged to have the couple's luggage pulled from the plane and stored in the baggage storage office until things calmed down. But her efforts on behalf of the Schmehlings didn't cease there. She went to visit Mrs. Schmehling in the hospital, and days later when Catherine was discharged, Aida picked up the Schmehlings at St. Mary's and drove them back to JFK airport for their return to St. Louis—all on her day off. And, of course, she took care of their luggage and arranged for a wheelchair for Catherine at Kennedy airport and back in St. Louis. Their tribulations, however, were not yet over. When they arrived at the airport, Catherine realized her x-rays had been left behind at the hospital. And of course, Aida again came to the rescue and arranged with the hospital to have the x-rays FedExed back home at TWA's expense.

Contributed by Susan Ahl

Beyond "Shirt Off Your Back" Service

Eric Nelson of Falls Church, VA, needed a replacement wheel for his damaged 1987 Volkswagen Fox. Nelson, a college senior, was in a hurry to get back to the University of Richmond for an important Monday morning class. He spent the better part of a Saturday fruitlessly searching the Falls Church area tire stores and junkyards looking for an inexpensive replacement. No one, it appeared, had a match in stock or could even make one available before Eric needed to be back at school.

Giving up on the used parts alternative, Nelson drove to Ray Burnette Volkswagon, in Alexandria, VA—a dealership he had contacted early in his search, and who he knew had a never-been-used-copy of the unusual wheel in stock. To his dismay, Nelson arrived an hour after the parts department had closed for the weekend—leaving only the sales staff on duty.

Undaunted, Nelson chased down a salesman and asked him if someone might have a key to the department; it was an emergency, Nelson pleaded. But the salesman said he couldn't help. Nelson pleaded some more, but the salesman still said he couldn't do it. As Nelson tried, to little avail, to change the salesman's mind, a man in a wheelchair quietly emerged from an adjacent office and asked Nelson what the problem was. When Nelson explained, the man ordered the salesman to remove a

wheel from a brand new VW Fox, which was sitting on the showroom floor, and then sell it to Nelson.

The order-giver was the man whose name was over the door: Ray Burnette. Ray's generosity and understanding only continued. The parts department computer couldn't be turned on because the office was locked, so there was no way to check the price of the new Fox wheel. Ray simply chose to believe him when Nelson attested he'd been quoted a price of $27 earlier.

"I've been in business for 45 years and I just try to help people," Ray says. "Since I didn't have the keys to the parts department, stripping a wheel off a showroom car was the only thing to do to help the young man out."

The Cable Guy Cometh ... and Serves

Take a roll call of recent complaints filed with the Better Business Bureau, and you'll likely turn up a rash of customers ticked off at the cable TV industry. Maybe you've experienced it yourself, or heard neighbors or the local newspaper tell the tales: tortoise-like repair service, missed appointment times, inability to talk live to service or technical support, and so on. Throughout the 1990s, in fact, cable service deteriorated so badly in parts of the country that local governments felt compelled to step in with regulations mandating new service standards.

No need for such intervention at Jones Intercable of Engle-wood, CO. Jones, one of the ten largest cable companies in the U.S. with 1.4 million customers, works hard—and creatively—to keep customers on its side. For one thing, Jones makes sure customer contact functions, including customer service installation and troubleshooting, are all handled at the local level, not from afar. For another, Jones' top management team places customer service high on its list of business imperatives, and evaluates performance accordingly.

Thanks to Tracy Hollingsworth, here are just a few of the ways the people at Jones Intercable are putting "service" back in the cable television business.

A customer phoned Jones Intercable in Englewood, CO, with an unusual holiday request. She had purchased a TV for her eleven-year-old son for Christmas, and wanted to give him a cable out-let in his room as well—so he could watch Nickelodeon and the Disney Channel whenever he wanted, away from the rest of the family. She also wanted this gift to be "From Santa," as would be the TV set. Aware that adding a cable outlet would require a house visit from a cable technician, she asked what Jones could do.

Turns out Jones was well up to the challenge. Techni-cian/installer Mark McCommas rented a Santa Claus costume and scheduled the install for just a few days prior to Christmas. The family, as well as a large group of neighborhood kids, were thrilled to see Santa Claus pull up into their driveway with an-other Jones technician dressed as an elf. Santa explained to the family's children that sometimes he gets to deliver gifts a little early, and proceeded to wire the outlet to the little boy's room.

Mark, the Jones installer, reports that Mom was so thrilled with the service she called the local radio station to file a long and glowing report about the event.

Contributed by Jana Henthorn

A major heavyweight boxing title fight had been scheduled for a Pay-Per-View showing on cable, and the Jefferson County Jones Intercable System in Colorado was preparing for very high service demand from its customers. In addition to making an extra number of "converter" boxes available for the demand, the cable system also ordered some programmable converters and other additional equipment.

But even after taking those precautionary measures, the supply of converter boxes ran out *four hours* before the fight was set to begin, with plenty of impatient customers left waiting to be hooked up.

General Manager Jim Honiotes and his staff brainstormed for a bit, and then settled on a set of novel solutions. He sent his entire cable staff home to collect the converter boxes off their own TV sets, and gave the boxes to 25 surprised and very grateful customers.

But the story gets even better. Those few customers who didn't get hooked up and were still unable to watch the fight at their homes were invited to a local tavern, where Jones Intercable paid for the Pay-Per-View event on the tavern's cable hook up, allowing all who wanted to see the fight to do so—on them.

Contributed by Jana Henthorn

Bill Wallace, a customer service technician for Jones Intercable in Independence, MO, answered a service call from Ms. Laplant, a new cable customer. Ms. Laplant was confused about her channel lineup. The problem, it turns out, was not very technical. As

Bill began walking Ms. Laplant through the maze of cable networks and channel numbers listed on her channel lineup card, it became obvious Ms. Laplant couldn't read the card because of her cataracts.

Undaunted, Bill returned to his office, enlarged the channel lineup card to 11" x 17" on the office copier, laminated it, and came back to hand-deliver it to the ecstatic Ms. Laplant.

Contributed by Rusty Robertson

Service providers who deal frequently with elderly or physically challenged customers often can get inured to complaints brought on by advancing age and other physical or emotional problems. But those who look a bit deeper, and don't write off these problems on first glance, can find some surprises—and rewards.

Robert Dinapoli, a longtime customer of Jones Intercable in Albuquerque, NM, suffers from spinal cerebellum degeneration, and is confined to a wheelchair. He also has some serious vision problems. When the picture on his TV set became too blurry for him to recognize, Robert called Jones Intercable to check on the cable line.

Taking the service call, Mike Mainolfa, a Jones technician in Albuquerque, NM, didn't write the complaint off out of hand—he wanted to make sure all bases were covered. Sure enough, with a bit of investigation he discovered that Robert's fifteen-year-old TV was the cause of the blurry picture, not his eyes.

With no money to buy a new TV set, Robert faced losing his "connection" to the community and much-valued entertainment. But he didn't count on Mike rallying his Jones associates, and the outpouring that followed.

"They bought me a brand new, 27" color TV with remote, all wrapped in a big ribbon," Robert wrote in a letter to a local Albuquerque paper. "I just can't get over it, to be honest."

Contributed by Steve Reifschneider

Carlson Companies: Where Over-the-Top Is Par for the Course

Carlson Companies Inc. is a diversified empire with operations at far corners of the globe, including some 1,100 hotel, resort, cruise ship, restaurant, and travel agency operations. But one overarching thread that ties these disparate Carlson units together is a concern for the customers' experience, and an enterprising spirit that ensures guests and clients walk away feeling they've been treated not as "one of many," but as distinct and valued customers.

If that feels a little grand for a $13.4 billion dollar company, witness these three Carlson employees who went above and beyond—in other words, met Carlson's minimum expectation for much of its customer contact staff—to ensure customer dazzlement.

Anyone who's frequented the casual, turn-of-the-century ambiance of a Carlson's T.G.I.F.'s (Friday's) restaurant knows to expect a lively atmosphere and top-of-the-line care. But one Friday's stunned even some seasoned restaurant-goers and ensured itself lifetime gold-medal status during the 1996 Summer Olympic Games in Atlanta.

In a letter to Friday's President and CEO Wallace Doolin, Queen Elizabeth II's representative at the Games, Sir Ian Michael Churchill, described the overwhelming service his party received at the T.G.I.F.'s in Gwinnett, GA, during their stay at the Games.

Here's an excerpt of Sir Ian's letter:

"A group numbering six—representing four countries and speaking just as many languages—had our evening meal at Friday's in Gwinnett, where we were served by a remarkable young man by the name of Harlan.

"As the host for this dinner, imagine my delight when Harlan turned to the two gentlemen from Barcelona and assisted in their selection, taking their order in perfect Spanish. Although fluent in English, the representative from Israel was thrilled when Harlan greeted him in a few words of Hebrew.

"The remainder of our party were two gentlemen from African colonies who spoke barely a word of English. At this point, Harlan produced a photo album of sorts, filled with pictures of the dishes found on Friday's menu. Upon closer examination of this pictorial menu, I discovered that there were symbols next to each photo, representing beef, chicken, fish, etc. Harlan informed me later that the idea and the assembly of this book were his own."

Birthday wishes do come true, especially if you're wishing for them at the Italianni's restaurant in Plymouth, MN, and your server is Deb Gordon. When a guest celebrating his birthday at the restaurant wished for a special dessert—an item not found on Italianni's regular dessert tray, but from another eating establishment altogether—Deb didn't flinch.

"We try to work by the G.R.A.N.D. philosophy here, which means `Guests Requests Are Never Denied,' Deb says. "When my customer said he wished he could get a Peanut Buster Parfait from Dairy Queen for his birthday dessert, I wanted to make sure he got his wish."

Deb told her manager about the request, and arrangements were made to hightail it to the nearest Dairy Queen to get the specified dessert. A short 15 minutes later, Deb presented the Peanut Buster Parfait to her stunned birthday guest.

"It was fun to see the look on his face," she says. "It made the dinner very special for him."

Contributed by Karen Waters

What kind of employee cancels weekend plans to deliver boxes of business documents to a client on the other side of the world? A Carlson Wagonlit Travel employee like David Fair, that's who. David did just that for Arthur Andersen & Co. when two boxes of training materials had to reach Malaysia in less than 48 hours.

It was late on a Friday afternoon and the Andersen Distribution Center (ADC) had to find a way to get sixty-six pounds of instructor guides to Kuala Lumpur for a training seminar the following Monday. Courier charges would have been $10,000—so the Carlson Wagonlit Travel team, which staff the Andersen Travel Center (ATC) in Chicago, IL, put their heads together to solve this logistics challenge.

"We decided our best course of action was to get someone on the next flight leaving for the Orient—which turned out to be in less than one hour," said Shari Palmer, the ATC/Carlson production supervisor. "So I asked for a volunteer with a passport, and David offered to go."

His roommate and the ADC manager met him at the gate with the Andersen materials and an overnight bag. David checked his bag and took the materials on board with him.

"All the way to London, he sat with the cases underfoot and his knees tucked up to his chin," said Palmer. With minutes to spare between flights in London, he had to leave his bag behind and dash through the airport with the materials in tow.

"This is a remarkable case, but a typical example of the team effort we see each day," said Mary Bastrentaz, a national travel manager for Arthur Andersen.

For David Fair and his ATC/Wagonlit colleagues, it was all in a day's work ... a very long day's work, for David.

Contributed by Nancy Pelant

Pitching In When the Unthinkable Happens

Only a parking lot separated the YMCA building from the truck-bomb explosion at the Alfred P. Murrah Federal Building in Oklahoma City, OK. But miraculously, everyone in the building survived the horrendous blast that killed 168 men, women, and children only a few short yards away. Other than blown out windows, the building looked intact from the outside. From the inside, the assessment was quite different. The interior was devastated—light fixtures were down, doors were blown away, and many interior walls had collapsed. Destroyed mechanical systems and broken glass covered the floor. And because it rained the afternoon after the blast, the building had experienced severe water damage.

Within 24 hours of the explosion, the St. Paul Companies, a Minnesota-based insurance company, received a claim from the YMCA, along with two dozen other claims related to the disaster. A team of St. Paul adjusters hopped on a plane to Oklahoma City to meet with customers and assess the extent of their losses. The Greater Oklahoma City Y—one of only two in the city—was particularly hard hit, and there was a pressing need to begin the clean up if the building was to be saved. Though authorities had roped off six blocks around the blast area to search for clues to the bombing, the St. Paul team negotiated access to the site and began their assessment of the damages while the FBI was still there, pulling bomb fragments from the walls.

Two days after the blast, national adjuster Ken Chapman—who had stayed at the site late into the night on that first day assessing the damage—delivered a $1 million advance payment to the YMCA to help alleviate the pressing need for cash to finance the work of boarding up 400 broken windows, stanching the water damage, and to begin rubble removal.

Local papers, such as *The Daily Oklahoman*, touted St. Paul's work with the YMCA as a "good example of how to help policyholders quickly get back on their feet, and reach amiable resolutions to some difficult claims. The advance was critical because it allowed the business to resume operation almost immediately."

Contributed by Jennifer Gatti

Neiman Marcus Makes Time for Service

It was two weeks before the opening of their new store in Minneapolis, MN, but at least one Neiman Marcus employee was ready to serve, regardless.

A panicked bridegroom called the store on Tuesday, four days before his wedding, asking for help in finding a tuxedo. Kevin Hoen, the men's wear department manager, didn't think twice about inviting the man into the store—even though building carpenters were still banging and hammering in preparation for the grand opening.

Before the groom-to-be's visit, Hoen made a round of calls and had an assortment of tuxedos, ties, shirts, and shoes emergency shipped to the as-yet-unstocked store. At 7 A.M. that Saturday, Hoen personally met with the customer in the makeshift departmental digs to finish outfitting.

Says Hoen of the episode, "It's not hard to get people to come into your store. The real trick is figuring out things you can do to keep them coming back—I'm sure he'll remember us in the future."

A Really Private Proposal

Marriage proposals in restaurants aren't exactly what you'd call unusual. But one went beyond business as usual when Paul Petrocci decided to pop the question to his girlfriend, Adrienne, in one of their favorite eateries, and do it in style.

Paul's plan was to ask Adrienne the ultimate question at lunch in the romantic ten-table loft section of a Smuggler's Restaurant in Tucson, AZ. When he disclosed his plan to the restaurant manager, things took a turn toward the memorable. Simply for the price of the meal, the manager arranged for Paul to have the section all to himself and an "Adrienne, will you marry me?" sign placed out front on the marquee. But when Paul and Adrienne arrived, they found the staff had just begun there. When they walked into the section they found that only one table occupied the roped-off loft, and along side it was a complimentary bottle of champagne. All the other tables had been cleared away.

And for the occasion, the restaurant staff had purchased special linen, china, silverware, and candelabras. Paul's tab? $13.00.

Contributed by Chip R. Bell

Pets and the People Who Love to Feed Them

The well-being of dogs and cats is an obsession at Hill's Pet Nu-trition, Inc., the Topeka, KS, manufacturer of Science Diet® and other specialty pet foods. In fact, the company was founded to further the work of a veterinarian, Mark Morris, Sr., who pio-neered the treatment of ill pets through diet. The company's cus-tomer care program is called the BUDDY system in honor and memory of Buddy, a German Shepherd who was one of the world's first seeing eye dogs. In 1943, Buddy developed kidney failure and Dr. Morris successfully treated him by changing the nutrient levels in his food. The pet foods and pet nutrition ser-vice Hill's offers today are direct descendants of Morris' original concept of nutrient balance. That focus on enriching the life and health of pets isn't lost on the current generation of Hill's service pros.

Dave Pedroza prides himself on taking good care of the cus-tomers on his route. He believes that the Prescription Diet® and Science Diet® pet foods he delivers to the veterinarians and pet stores in his Northern Illinois territory are as important to the fi-

People and their Pets

nancial health of his customers as the products are to the health of pets that consume them. He thinks of his customers as "partners in pet nutrition."

So when he realized that several thousand pounds of product slated for Regole's Harvest Shoppe in St. Charles, one of his biggest customers, was being backordered—and backordered "just-in-time" for Regole's owner Mary Ann Miller's annual sale—he became Dave Pedroza, Super Scrounge!

Pedroza finished his day's deliveries in near record time, and was back in the Hill's service center warehouse with a mission in mind. Regole's order in hand, he went through every truck in the lot piecing together the order one bag at a time from the overages and undelivered stock of the other route managers.

Don't, however, suggest that Pedroza was involved in a nasty act of "midnight requisition and supply." Says Dave, "It was all on the up and up, but I went through every Hill's truck on the lot and located all the one offs I needed to make up the order. I took the product and left notes for the other drivers letting them know what I had to do." He loaded his truck and returned to Regole's Harvest Shoppe delivering the product the same day! Mary Ann was ecstatic to see the entire order come through her door in ample time for the sale. Of his exemplary service to customers like Miller, Dave simply says, "I treat my customers like they are king, and in turn, they roll out the red carpet for me. To make it even better, I am really having fun! This is a great feeling!"

Lori Smith, a Hill's customer service rep in Topeka, KS, received a phone call on an 800 line from a distressed pet owner in Texas. The woman's twelve-year-old cocker spaniel was not expected to live through the night, due to a severe heart condition. Just before leaving the university medical school veterinary center, the owner had received one of Hill's special dietary foods to feed her ailing pet, in the event that it survived the night—a hope the vet had cautioned against.

When morning came, the woman called Hill's directly to discuss the use of the special food, as her dog had indeed defied the odds. As it turned out, the vet had given the dog a reformulated pet food that hadn't actually been put in distribution yet.

So Lori calculated the feeding requirements for the dog; believing the dog might survive longer than a day or two, Lori began searching for more of the reformulated product for the dog.

After a number of dead-end phone calls to her usual sources in the company—and nearly an hour's effort—she finally found someone who knew of the product and could act as a source for the new formula if the Texas woman's dog continued to defy the odds.

By the end of that same day Lori and her new found confederate had rounded up two cases of the reformulated product, and had arranged to have it shipped overnight—at no expense to the customer, of course.

Contributed by Kathy Davis

6 P.M. Whistle Doesn't Slow Down These Kaset Employees

At Kaset International Corp., working across divisional or departmental boundaries isn't the teeth-pulling and divisive exercise it can be at some other companies. When the chips are down and a customer needs help, it seems there are few barriers to employees working together, and little evidence of the "it's not my job" flu bug.

A case in point, Marcia Wilson, an employee in Kaset's energy division, was wrapping up work one day at 6:15 P.M. when she heard a nearby phone ring. She could have easily let the call roll over to night messaging, but instead picked it up. The call was from a panicked customer who had forgotten to order some materials for a training session—some facilitator guides—scheduled for 8:30 A.M. the next morning.

Marcia took the information calmly, reassured the customer that everything would be fine, and hung up. Then she wondered how on earth she would follow through on her promise.

After a few calls to inform co-workers of the situation, Marcia paged Lisa Powers in the Kaset logistics department, not expecting to find her. Powers, also on her way out of the building, took the information about the customer, knowing just enough about the account to understand which materials the customer needed. She also knew there were no facilitator guides available for this customer. In fact, she had just sent the masters to the print shop to replenish the inventory.

Powers promptly called the night shift of company's copy center, explained the dilemma, and asked if they could produce five guides ASAP. She then made some calls to determine the address of the customer's training site, since the customer hadn't left the correct address. (Meanwhile, another Kaset employee, Lorraine Bello, had again contacted the customer to reassure him everything was okay.)

Powers made arrangements for a courier to pick up the facilitator guides when they were ready at 9:30 P.M., and to drive them to the customer's training site—some eight hours away.

When the customer arrived the next morning, there was the courier on the door step, waiting with the prized materials.

Contributed by Lisa Night

Delta People Love to Fly—And This One Loves to Serve

Susan A. Poindexter is a senior customer services agent at one of Delta's offices in Cincinnati, OH. Susan was on duty one day in 1987 when a woman traveling with two small children became ill during a stop in the city. The woman, who spoke no English, needed to go to the hospital. What to do? Point to the cab stand? Call a skycap? Plead ignorance of the strange language and hope someone else would take charge? Poindexter went above and beyond. She accompanied the woman and her children to the hospital. When the woman was released, she took the travelers home with her and put them up overnight. The next day, she took them back to the airport and got them boarded for home.

If Asked Nicely, He May Even Do Windows

Mark Hayes, a customer accounts field rep with Water District No. 1 of Johnson County, KS, was on a trip to the home of an elderly customer who was confused about her water bill, and some other household management issues.

After talking the customer through her problems, Mark noticed her yard was completely overgrown with grass and weeds. Knowing that this particular city had an ordinance requiring neatly trimmed lawns, he was concerned that the customer might be cited and fined, not to mention get her share of guff from her neighbors. So he took it upon himself to research the cheapest source of lawn mowing service in the area, and arranged to have a service come by and take care of the customer's lawn.

Says Mark's supervisor, Mike Brewer, "The action was taken with little expectation of reward or notice, and probably would have gone completely unnoticed, except that the lawn care provider was so impressed that he contacted the Water board chairman to report it. Mark's a pretty good guy, isn't he?"

Contributed by Mike Brewer

Nordstrom Strikes Again

While on assignment in Seattle, WA, Fran Sims, a St. Petersburg, Florida-based consultant, had bought a bathing suit from the downtown flagship location of Nordstrom's department store. The sales reps bagged the suit, and graciously accepted Sim's out-of-state check for payment—itself no small indicator of service sensitivity.

But when Sims returned to her hotel room, she found a message. The Nordstrom rep had inadvertently left one of the swimming suit straps out of Sims' bag, and wanted to personally deliver it to her hotel. Sims wondered how the rep had tracked her down. "You remember I asked you to write the name of your company on the back of your check?," the rep said. "I called Florida information to get the phone number for your company, called them, and asked where you were staying in town."

Sims thanked the rep and said she could just leave the strap at her hotel's front desk. The rep insisted that since she was responsible for leaving the strap out of the bag, she should deliver it personally to Sims.

Neither Rain Nor Wind Nor High Tide Stays These Service Detectives

A few years ago, Atlanta-based Shop'n Chek, which "shops" or sends its representatives undercover to measure the service quality of client companies, created a "mystery shopping" program for a national car manufacturer. As part of its service, Shop'n Chek guaranteed 100% completion of all their mystery shopping visits by a certain date. In this case, all the promised shops on all the designated auto dealerships had been completed—with the exception of the visit scheduled for the one lone dealership on Martha's Vineyard, a popular resort island off the coast of Cape Cod, MA.

According to COO Cleve Rowley, the weather was so horrendous that ice and snow were preventing the normally reliable car ferry from running out to the island. "It really seemed like there was no way our shopper could get out to the Island to perform the shop," he says. Still, Shop'n Chek had promised the client that all shops would be completed, and they felt driven to honor that promise.

The solution? Shop'n Chek chartered a plane and flew the designated shopper safely out to Martha's Vineyard, where he hopped out of the plane, walked to the dealership, completed his shop—and lived up to the company promise.

Contributed by Cleve Rowley

Domino's Delivers

A spouse's worst nightmare: stranded on Valentine's Day. Such was the case with Mr. Grasso of Ramsey, NJ. Stuck in an airport hundreds of miles from home, with no chance of getting a flight back until the next day, the 15th, Grasso knew a simple "I'm sorry, Honey," wouldn't make up for the lost romantic evening he and his wife had planned. He needed more.

He started by calling Domino's Customer Care Center to find the Domino's store nearest his home. They pointed him toward store #3972 in his home town of Ramsey, NJ, who he called to explain that he was stranded, and could they deliver a pizza to his wife and charge it to his credit card? Store manager Dan Trumbauer took Mr. Grasso's order and asked if there was anything else he could do. Grasso jokingly said, "Maybe flowers on the box!" Inspired by the off-handed remark, Trumbauer did just that—he went to a nearby flower shop and bought a bouquet. Then he personally delivered the pizza and the bouquet of flowers to Mrs. Grasso.

Mr. Grasso was so impressed when he learned of Trumbauer's thoughtful gesture that he called the Customer Care Center back and told them that he wanted to tell the world about this wonderful piece of above and beyond service.

Contributed by Sharon Ceci

Going "Above and Beyond" for the Boys from Down Under

Often going above and beyond for a customer is motivated by nothing more complex nor less noble than a desire to save the day for someone in desperate need of a break. Such was the case for a team of Good Samaritans from Professional Travel Corporation (PTC) in Denver, CO, when they conspired to come to the rescue of a pair of hapless would-be world travelers from Australia. In the words of J.D. Ralls and Jan Lunquist of PTC we bring you the following scenario.

The Saga of Maurice and Giavanni

"Maurice and Giavanni set out for a vacation of a lifetime— an around-the-world excursion with stops in North America, Europe, and Asia before returning home to Australia. Many of their friends had ventured out on similar trips, coming home with talk of wonderful and exciting experiences in the United States. The U.S. was Maurice's and Giavanni's first destination, and they had high expectations of the sojourn.

"When the plane touched down on the Los Angeles runway, Maurice and Giavanni quickly grabbed their carry-on bags in hopes of being first off the plane. They could hardly wait to see America and to begin their adventure. Little did they know. Step one was finding a hotel.

"Since many hotels are located just outside of the Los Angeles airport, they didn't expect a problem. Maurice and Giavanni claimed their luggage and were about to cross the street when a car approached rapidly. Maurice thought he saw a gun pointed at them. Scared, Giavanni yelled 'RUN.' The car chased after them and caused the guys to split up. Poor Giavanni. In an effort to elude his pursuers he ran down an alley and jumped into a trash dumpster, where he ended up spending the night—fearful for his life. He was simply too afraid to climb out of the dumpster until dawn. Maurice's only good luck was to find a police station.

"Seriously afraid for his friend, the officers immediately assisted Maurice in locating Giavanni. By now many hours had passed so the search began at the airport. Fortunately, Giavanni was found alive, well, and with a very strong odor about him thanks to the dumpster.

"Escorted by the officers, Maurice and Giavanni arrived safely at a hotel. They thanked the officers, checked into the hotel and discussed how America was such a big disappointment. How could their friends have led them to believe what a great country this was? Were there many Americans out there like these men? They decided to leave the United States as soon as possible.

"The following morning they found PTC's phone number in the telephone listings, after being unable to reach their airline. They called PTC to change their airline tickets and to end their nightmare. They were going home! Jan Lunquist, who took their call, was horrified when she learned that Maurice and Giavanni actually believed all Americans could be like those men. She got their telephone number at the Los Angeles hotel, obtained approval to change their tickets without any additional charges, and had Maurice and Giavanni scheduled on a flight within the next two hours. She advised them of their new flight plans, wished them well, and ended the call. But it didn't feel right to her. She felt she just could have done more.

"So Jan then turned to co-worker J.D. Ralls and told her Maurice and Giavanni's story. Jan asked J.D. if perhaps she would be interested in helping her show a couple of Australians what American hospitality was really like. Jan wanted Maurice and Giavanni to leave the United States with a positive impression, and knowing that there were many kind-hearted and loving people living here.

"J.D. was free over the weekend, so Jan called Maurice and Giavanni at their hotel, only to find out they had just checked out. Jan had scheduled them on a connection through Denver so she next called the airline.

"Maurice and Giavanni had already checked in for their flight. After explaining the situation, Jan was able to convince an airline employee to contact the boarding area of their flight to have Maurice and Giavanni paged. Giavanni came to the phone and Jan extended her invitation. She advised Giavanni they were welcome to stay with she and Fred, and then Jan, J.D., and Fred would show them a little of America's "wild, wild west." Giavanni and Maurice eagerly accepted. They boarded their flight and headed for Denver.

"The next challenge for Jan was to talk to the Denver airline personnel because Maurice's and Giavanni's luggage would need to be taken off the plane upon arrival. This was not a normal procedure for the airline.

"Jan and J.D. went to the airport on their lunch hour to welcome Maurice and Giavanni to Denver. Jan successfully arranged for their luggage to be taken off the flight. Maurice and Giavanni were then taken back to Professional Travel where their tickets were changed once again, and to wait for Jan and J.D. to finish their work day.

"For the next two days, Jan and J.D., Maurice and Giavanni, and sundry friends and family made Denver their oyster: sightseeing, four-wheeling, and doing what the local folks do. By Sunday evening Maurice and Giavanni were convinced that Colorado was not only beautiful, but one of the best places to live in the world. They now even believed America was as great as their friends had said. Maurice and Giavanni left the United States with the longing to someday return."

Contributed by Jan Lunquist and J.D. Ralls

2

Great Saves

Great saves. Snatching victory from the jaws of defeat. Service recovery.

Call it what you will, some of the most memorable stories of great service begin with the sounds of service breakdown—that all-too-familiar clatter that happens every time a customer's experience falls short of his or her expectations. The waiter moves in slow motion; the doctor sees you at 11:30 A.M. for your 9:30 A.M. appointment; the flight is late; the laundry cracks all the buttons on your best blouse; the phone goes dead mid-call; the cable keeps presenting Olga's Russian Calisthenics Hour every time you turn to the place on the dial where HBO should be. In the end you walk away disgruntled and angered by the dissonance between the actual and the expected experience. And sometimes you vow never to return. And sometimes you even don't.

The technical term for turning customer disappointment into delight is "recovery," a term deliberately taken from the medical language. Recovery denotes the things you do to restore a customer to a state of equanimity with your organization. Recovery is about making customers whole again; about helping them regain and reclaim what they feared was lost forever. An economic recovery is an upturn in finances, a service recovery is an upturn in spirits; a renewal of faith and trust in you and your organization.

Note those last 4 words: *You And Your Organization.*

Any customer service person with half an ounce of cleverness can easily turn away an upset customer's wrath by siding with him, "Oh, I know. It's just terrible. If it was up to me, I'd give you the money back right now. But *they've* got this policy and if I break it, well—you know!" That, of course, gets the rep off the spot, but does nothing to repair—and indeed actually worsens—the customer's view of the organization.

This chapter is about Great Saves. People who did the right things for their troubled customers, and did them in a way that restored their customers' faith in both the organization and the service people themselves; acts of service recovery that not only solved the customer's problem, but that honored the server, the served, and the organization.

Say It With Service

Good friends of ours were celebrating their 25th wedding anniversary. We called to congratulate them, and to check on the flowers we'd ordered for their big day—and for the big party they were having that evening. To our chagrin, what had arrived was hardly the large pair of festive arrangements we had envisioned—it was, instead, a puny potted plant. An itsy-bitsy, teeny thing that, at best, might brighten some little corner of the half bath off their family room.

It was after 6 P.M. and their party was set for 7:30 P.M. We called and caught Jerry at Lindskoog Florists on his way out the door, and explained the foul up. "Don't say another word," he advised, "I'll fix this right now." At 7:10 P.M. our friends called back to tell us that a truck had just delivered two magnificent arrangements and a center piece for their buffet table. Oh—did I mention? Our friends live in North Carolina—and we, and our florist, live in Minneapolis, one time zone and half a continent away.

When the bill arrived it was for the cost of our original order only, and was hand delivered by Jerry the florist with hat—and a small arrangement—in hand. He apologized again for the problem, and assured us it would not happen again. No excuses. No passing the blame to the fulfilling florist in Charlotte. No "You can't believe the kind of help I have to deal with today." No nothing; just—"Once again, I'm sorry for the problem. I hope you will think of us again when you think of flowers." And you can bet we will. And have.

A Simple Moral

Texas A&M marketing professor Leonard Berry has studied service quality longer and more thoroughly than anyone I know. He sums up the esteem you and I have for the Jerry's of the world in one wonderfully simple, yet elegant sentence:

> "The acid test of service quality is how well you solve your customer's problems."

The mythical Dr. Murphy's famous warning is as apt for the 1990s as it was for 1960s, "Anything that can go wrong, will go wrong." In today's marketplace, shrugging your shoulders and accepting errors and mess ups as inevitable is an unacceptable risk. You need every customer you have. And you'll need them tomorrow as well as today. And the day after that, and the day after that, and the day after that as well—if you intend to be in business for the long haul. That means recovering well—no, make that spectacularly—when customer problems arise.

As with any other aspect of exceptional service, solving customer problems adroitly is more than a strategy or a set of skills. It is a way of life. It is part of the culture of organizations that serve customers well day in and day out.

Ron Zemke

Service with a Smell: Going Where Few Have Gone Before...

It wasn't the fault of the Peachtree Center in Atlanta, GA, that Jennifer Stein parked her car where she did. But when Stein got out of that car to do some shopping and dropped her keys— right through the sewer grating at her feet—the service people at the Center knew they had to do something to change Jennifer's day from rotten to recovered.

Receiving a call from security, engineers Randy McCarty, Ronnie Milam, and Richard Burns all swung into action. They arrived at the scene, removed the drain cover, and surveyed the situation. It didn't take long for them to determine that retrieving the keys would mean a good portion of the foul-smelling, garbage-laden water laying fallow in the drain would have to be bailed out.

Milam took a deep breath and gamely crawled down with a bucket. He filled it and handed it up to his partners to be emptied. Two hours later he was able to feel around in the sludge with his hands and locate the keys. Stein was elated.

To express her appreciation, she offered twenty dollars to the engineers, which they promptly turned down. "It isn't every day you find people as helpful and willing as these gentlemen," Stein wrote in a letter of thanks to Peachtree's general manager. "It sure is great when you do."

L.L. Bean ... Again

L.L. Bean's reputation for service recovery has reached almost mythical proportions in the United States. But Karen Larson, a consultant in Maple Grove, MN, says the company's penchant for exceeding expectations is rooted firmly in reality.

Larson recently sent back to L.L. Bean a shirt she had purchased that had worn out after many years of hard use. The shirt had frayed at the cuffs in an unusual way, and Larson thought the company "might be interested in that kind of product information from a customer. I made it clear in my letter that I was not looking for any sort of compensation from them," she says.

Not long afterward, Larson received a phone call from an L.L. Bean customer service rep, who told her the company would like to replace the shirt, but no longer carried it in the color she had originally purchased.

"Although I made it clear I wasn't expecting a replacement, it seemed important to her," Larson says. So Larson gave the rep her color preference and size information. The rep then told her the shirt was on sale for half price, so L.L. Bean would be sending two shirts to her—at no cost.

"Just as I was thinking the company has managed to exceed my already high expectations," Larson says, "they did one more thing. A few days after I got the shirts in the mail, I received a check to cover the postage cost I had incurred when mailing the original shirt."

Of Cabs and Planes and Sealing Wax and Hotel Rooms for Kings

Our partner, Chip Bell, is a bonafide first-class Service Magnet, who seems at times to get better service than almost anyone in the Western world. Of course he is always and forever finding himself in odd and unusual situations where it takes great service to get him where he needs to go or accomplish what he needs done. Perhaps it's his hectic and frenetically paced work life. Perhaps it's his whirlwind, high-energy personality. Whatever the case and cause, stories of great service follow him—particularly those we call Great Saves. Here are two of our favorite Chip Bell stories—and if you look carefully, you just might find one or two more in later chapters.

Sometimes great service pops up in unexpected quarters. As this story reminds us, great saves are not the sole proviso of Fortune 500 companies, upscale hotels, or famous department stores. But what follows, in Chip's own words, was a real surprise example.

"The flight out of Las Vegas would be full; they always are on Sunday nights. As my taxi weaved through traffic, I realized that not only was I cutting it close on time, I had a reservation but no seat assignment. Without a seat, I was at risk of getting bumped. With a nervous quiver in my voice, I beseeched the driver to ask his radio dispatcher to call the airline and try to get me a seat assignment.

"Are you kidding me?" said the driver. "Our dispatcher services three cab companies and over five hundred cabs. She'll just laugh if I even ask."

"Please try it," I persisted. He did—in one of those "You won't believe what this guy is asking for" tones of voice. I was beginning to feel I was barking up a very wrong tree.

"But the dispatcher for Yellow-Checker-Star cab companies fooled us both. She responded to my desperate request with such great calmness and confidence, I would have thought she got several hundred such requests a week. After a brief pause, she gave me an assignment. "I need the passenger's help," she typed to the taxicab computer. "Please give me the destination, flight number, and the airline's phone number if you have it." I wheeled into action with all the requested information.

"Time passed as we sped toward McCarran International. In a few minutes a message appeared on the cab driver's computer screen: "The airline has put me on hold, will advise." I was starting to be very impressed and assured that a pro was on my case. A minute later, the message came back. "Too late to get a seat, the airline says the flight has been delayed and you should be just fine. Good luck. I hope you make it all right!"

"This is amazing," mumbled the driver, overwhelmed by the dispatchers tenacity and determination. I asked the driver for the dispatcher's name. Thank you, Rebecca Thomas! You made a hectic business trip to Las Vegas end on a very positive note by partnering with me under extraordinary pressure."

The Marriott Long Wharf in Boston was full—chocked full— with no room in the inn at any price. And at the late hour Chip arrived, even the emergency rooms, given to the late, late arrivals were gone. But the Marriott had a recovery plan in place for such occasions, and Jan Blum, the front desk manager, came to the rescue, "I'm sorry Dr. Bell, but we are entirely sold out— and I know you had a guaranteed reservation. However, I know

that there are some rooms available at our Copley Plaza Hotel. Here is a note to the night manager and my business card. I'll call ahead and tell them you are coming. And here is twenty dollars which should cover the cost of the cab ride over there tonight and back here tomorrow. I promise we'll have a room ready and waiting for you when you arrive back here after your business is done for the day. And again, I'm very sorry for the inconvenience, Dr. Bell."

We were all impressed by that splendid example of service recovery. We were even more impressed with what happened to Chip the next time he checked into the Marriott Long Wharf a few week's later. We pick up the story in Chip's own words.

"The same front desk manager, Jan Blum, was about to 'walk' me again to another hotel because an earlier power outage nearby had forced several hotels to divert their arriving guests to the Marriott, which did have power. Realizing my past patience would likely turn into ire if I were bumped again, Blum said with a twinkle in his eye, "I have a surprise for you! We never use Room 500 in overbooked situations like this. But you are a special guest, it's very late, and you are only here for one evening. I want you to get Room 500. I will be on duty in the morning as you check out, and I'll be very anxious to get your reaction to this unusual room."

"Even the bellman looked surprised as I handed him my luggage and the key to Room 500. The mystery room turned out to be a gigantic, two-bedroom penthouse suite with a panoramic view of the Boston harbor, a sunken living room with fireplace, grand piano, library—the works.

"I immediately regretted that it was close to midnight and that I was only staying for one evening."

Ron Zemke

George Jetson—and Wendy's—to the Rescue

Though fast-food drive-thrus are somewhat notorious for causing service headaches, a Wendy's in Minneapolis made some lasting friends with its response to a six-year-old who didn't receive her promised Jetson's cup, part of a restaurant promotion.

Although it's probably the type of problem many customers would ignore, Gretchen Olesen's mom decided it was time to see if fast-food restaurants really do care about their customers.

When Ms. Olesen got home and noticed her daughter's cup was missing, she called the restaurant and asked them to mail it. Although the store's management promised to do so, two weeks went by with no cup. Gretchen's growing disappointment was enough to urge her mother to take up pen and write Wendy's then-CEO, Robert Barney, and explain the incident.

About 10 days later, Wendy's customer service department delivered not just one Jetson's cup, but a set of them with a letter of apology—and coupons for two free meals. That same evening, Frank Kline, Wendy's local director of area operations, stopped by the Olesen's house to personally apologize and deliver two more Jetson's cups.

But it was the final letter, personally addressed to Gretchen, that really did the trick. George Jetson himself and his dog, Astro, wrote to reassure her that Wendy's wasn't trying to cheat her, and that they were sorry she hadn't gotten her cup right away. Astro even included his pawprint for a signature.

"Gretchen was so excited that she took the letter to school and had her teacher read it to her class," her mother reports. "There are probably about twenty first graders and even a few teachers who are more frequent visitors to Wendy's these days."

Dogged Pursuit of Customer Satisfaction Wins National Car Rental a Customer for ... Eternity

If at first you don't recover, try and try again. And yet again. That was the modus operandi of National Car Rental as it refused to give up its pursuit of a happy end for a disgruntled customer.

Ray Brook, a product supply market manager at Procter & Gamble and a frequent National Car Rental customer, was more than a little puzzled when a remote rental machine at the Portland, OR, airport rejected his request for a car and requested he see an agent at the main terminal. The National Car agent quickly found the problem: Brook's Washington-state driver's license had expired on his birthday just the week before. Due to some sticky liability issues, National couldn't rent him a car without a valid license.

With the prospect of meeting a customer in 30 minutes and a full day of business 600 miles away in Sacramento, CA, facing him the next day, Brook was frantic. Wayne Ranslem, National's on-duty manager, was summoned, and confirmed the company's policy on licenses. Ranslem could have let the exchange end there. Instead, he offered to drive Brook to his customer meeting—20 minutes away—and then to the Department of Motor Vehicles (DMV) to renew his license—another 30 minute drive. Another National employee fulfilled the chauffeuring duties as Brook accepted the generous offer.

But his travails weren't over. The DMV office was closed.

Back went Brook and the driver to the Portland airport, where National's Ranslem laid out Plan B. National would transport Brook to his hotel where he would take responsibility for his own transportation for the rest of today. Another National employee would pick him up early the next morning and take him back to Vancouver, WA, for the renewal, after which he could rent a car—at a discount—for the trip to Sacramento. This time, finally, everything went according to plan.

In a follow-up letter to National's CEO, Vince Wasik, Brook wrote, "It's apparent this kind of persistence in customer service only happens as the result of very strong leadership, clear direction, and discipline in key principles. My sincere thank you to you and your organization for providing that."

Playing by Stew's Rules

Stew Leonard's Dairy Store in Norwalk, CT, has long been notorious for the lengths it goes to put smiles on customers' faces.
Passing out free cookies and ice cream to people who have to
wait more than 5 minutes in line before checking out, and keeping at least two-thirds of the store's checkstands open all the
time so those treats usually aren't necessary, are just a few of
the little things the store does to set itself apart. Maybe the
biggest reason Stew Leonard's still overflows with stories of out-
of-the-ordinary service feats and great saves is that store management goes out of its way to reward initiative on the part of
employees.

Take these three never-say-die Leonard's staffers, for instance.

A few years back a woman wandered up to a young man who
had just started working in Stew Leonard's Lost and Found Department, and inquired whether a gold Cross pen had turned
up. It seemed the pen had been her father's, and he had since
passed away, and she was feeling a little down and out because
of the sentimental value attached. She wasn't even sure she'd
lost it in the store, she confessed, but the young man dutifully
went from department to department, returning after a while to
report he'd had no success in turning up the pen.

Here's where the story gets even better. Noticing that the
woman was just about in tears by now, the young man reached
down under the counter, pulled out three $20 gift certificates (a
gold Cross pen costs about $15 to $20, in case you're wondering) signed them, and handed them to her, saying that he knew
they couldn't replace what the pen had meant to her, but he'd
keep looking and meanwhile, maybe this would make her feel
a bit better.

After the woman left, it occurred to him that, since he was
new, maybe he should make sure he had done the right thing in
giving away the store's money like that. So he sought out Stew
Leonard, Jr., and described what had happened. You be the
manager for a moment—how would you have reacted? The
younger Leonard took prompt and decisive action.

First, he put the story in the next issue of *Stew's News*, the store's monthly newsletter, with the young man's picture and a glowing description of how he'd done something on behalf of a customer. Second, he gave him a $600 scholarship to attend a Dale Carnegie course because, as he told us, "That's a skill we want developed in our organization."

It's a Friday afternoon at Leonard's when one of management's ultimate fears becomes reality: a computer failure shuts down all the grocery's cash registers. Most customers wait patiently alongside their filled grocery carts, but one very agitated customer leaves, drives 30 minutes to get home, then calls to complain to the manager that because of the computer crash, she has no groceries for her husband George's 60th birthday party— and she refuses to shop anywhere else but Stew Leonard's grocery.

Within an hour, a car pulls up at her house and out pops a Stew Leonard's employee who delivers the groceries—which had been dictated from a list over the phone. But he's also toting a birthday cake that says, "Happy 60th George. Sincerely, Stew." Any wonder the customer says she wouldn't think about shopping elsewhere?

A customer stalks up to Leonard's customer service desk, slams down two empty cases of pop cans, and impatiently announces to Marion Murphy, who happens to be on duty there at the time, that he doesn't have time to feed twenty-four cans, one-by-one, into an automatic recycling machine—and he wants his money back right now. Marion explains that this isn't the can-return department, but since he's in a hurry she'll be happy to get the money out of her purse and feed the machine on her own lunch break to get reimbursed. Nonplused, the customer asks if she's serious. She says yes, it's her job to keep customers happy. The man blushes, picks up the cans, and takes them over to the machine after telling her, "If you've got the time, I've got the time."

Just the Fax, Ma'am: Victimized by a Paper Landslide

Fax subscribers to Sarah Stambler's newsletter, *Marketing with Technology News*, arrived in their offices one day to find their fax machines spitting out a seemingly endless stream of blank paper. Through an unexplained technological glitch in the file conversion software of SprintFax—the company that "broadcast" the newsletter to subscribers—a 100-page blank file was sent out with the newsletter.

It got even worse for some unlucky customers. In some cases, when the system failed to deliver all 100 pages on the first try, it resent the file, so some subscribers actually got more than 100 blank pages.

According to *Hotline*, a publication of the Newsletter Publishing Association (NPA), nearly 300 subscribers were caught in the paper avalanche. "Our phone was just ringing off the hook once the business day began," Stambler told *Hotline*. One angry customer, bent on retaliation against the newsletter, set up an endless paper loop of his own designed to fax Stambler's office into infinity.

But by 2 P.M. the day after the disaster, Sprintfax, the broadcast fax company, had shifted full force into a recovery mode. All affected customers were faxed a gushing letter of explanation and apology, offered two free rolls of fax paper and a coupon for 30 minutes free phone time for their personal use.

"What began as an absolute nightmare turned into a positive event thanks to the quick corrective action taken by Sprint-Fax," says Stambler.

Good Enough? Let It Slide?
Not in Ed Lennon's World, You Don't!

Ed Lennon, an installer for Southern New England Telephone (SNET) who works out of Hamden, CT, is another example of someone doing just that little bit more, which separates adequate service recovery from the truly outstanding and memorable variety. One Friday, after finishing the interior installation work for a new business scheduled to celebrate its grand opening the following Monday, he called in to activate the hookup. No way, he was told, the crew responsible for that part of the job had been unable to do its work because construction on the property hadn't been properly finished off. Even worse, the crew had left the site without talking to any of the contractors who might have been able to correct the situation while putting the finishing touches on the building. The crew now was unavailable until Monday—which meant the company would be without phones up to and including the moment of its grand opening.

Lennon could have punched out, gone home, and let the system run on its own momentum. He didn't. The customer was startled the following morning, when a SNET truck pulled up and a crew started installing the lines. Shortly thereafter, Lennon stopped by to check things out. It turned out he had talked to his foreman about the situation, and they had found a way to get a crew in on Saturday, and the phones switched on that same day, saving the customer from the embarrassment of opening for business—without really being open for business.

She "Hurried on Down to Hardees," and They Hurried on Down to Her!

As a regular break during its busy season, when overtime is piling up, the staff of the Graduate School Admissions Office at Duke University in Durham, NC, treat themselves to a group breakfast on Saturday mornings. This particular Saturday it was Donna Lee Giles' turn to get the treats, and she chose a local Hardee's.

Giles placed her order for twenty-six dollars worth of goodies, was waited on promptly, and left quickly with the bag of food. But when she arrived at the office, she found a disturbing number of errors in the order—mistakes in the biscuits, and none of the six orders had the hash `rounds' she had ordered. Peeved, she called the restaurant to complain. Based on her previous experience with some fast food outlets, she wasn't expecting much in the way of sympathy—or corrective action.

But Steve Craddock, manager of the Hardee's on Guess Road in Durham, had other things in mind. He had a very unhappy customer on his hands, and that wouldn't do. He picked up the missing items and drove out to deliver them personally to Giles' office—along with some complimentary cinnamon biscuits for their inconvenience.

Shortly after Steve's delivery, Giles received a phone call from the young woman who had waited on her, who proceeded to apologize for her mistake.

In a follow-up letter to Hardees's, Giles could hardly contain her praise. "Here is a manager who takes customer service very seriously, who seems to instill in his people a sense of personal responsibility. Keep Mr. Craddock, promote him, let him train others—your business needs people like him, and consumers need people like him."

Contributed by Boddie Noell Franchise

Fly in Your Soup? How About a Latex Glove in Your Stir Fry?

"High performance customer service," as Richard Porter likes to call memorable transactions, doesn't come often, but it came to him one cold winter's day in Toronto, Canada, and it was indeed unforgettable.

We'll let Richard tell it in his own voice, as he did in *Chicken Soup for the Soul at Work:*

"My wife Kate and I had a weekend alone. Saturday was an exercise in leisure and tranquillity; we got up late, and everything in the day was a pleasurable three or four hours late.

"After browsing shops and galleries, we arrived at a prominent four-star hotel at around four o'clock, ready for a late lunch. The restaurant staff was most accommodating. Kate ordered a stir-fry of some sort, and when it arrived, the real adventure began.

"Nestled neatly in Kate's stir-fry was the tip of a finger from a latex glove. I called the waitress. "What is this?" Kate inquired with an appropriate level of indignation.

"I'm not sure," replied the waitress as she whisked the plate away to the kitchen.

"In less than a minute the waitress returned with the maitre d'. "Madame, we have made a dreadful mistake and apologize sincerely." So far, so good. "Let us start over," the maitre d' continued. "Remove everything from the table," he instructed the waitress. The waitress proceeded to remove everything—the wine, the cutlery, my food, the tablecloth—everything! "Let us erase the memory," said the maitre d'.

"The table was reset, menus presented again, and new wine and food ordered. We were on our way once again to a fantastic lunch. The maitre d' took a bad service impression and replaced it with an outstanding one. He did not deny the experience, but substituted a higher, richer one in its place."

Contributed by Richard Porter

How Bell Canada Taketh and Then Giveth Away Its Phone Service

Arrange to have a new phone line installed, and usually your biggest concern is the technician arriving at the appointed time. You don't generally expect he'll take away your existing phone service, too.

Nigel Mahabir, a customer client representative for Bell Canada in Scarborough, Ontario, had spoken to a customer and arranged for the connection of new phone lines in her home. The company sent a business technician out to hook up her new lines. But instead, he mistakenly deactivated the existing lines and facilities.

When Nigel made his above and beyond the call-of-duty follow-up call to check on the quality of the installation service, he discovered to his horror—and to the customer's growing dismay—what had happened. Feeling responsible, he took immediate ownership of the problem, and arranged for a quick return visit to shore up the damage.

Unfortunately, it was about that same time one of the biggest snowstorms of the season had swung into high gear, making the repair near impossible. But Nigel and his colleagues weren't calling it a day. "There was no way we could allow this woman and her family to be without phone service," Nigel says.

After finishing his own shift at 8 P.M., Bell Canada senior associate Richard Clarke, who had been consulting with Nigel, drove an hour and a half through a blinding snowstorm to give the customer his personal cellular phone to use until her service was restored.

A few days later, after the storm had abated and the customer's service reconnected, Richard followed up to ensure everything was okay. When he called, the customer had just finished talking to the local newspaper, with whom she happily shared tales of Bell Canada's persistence at making things right—and Clarke's heartwarming trust in loaning her his personal phone.

Contributed by Mary Ann Monas and Michael Corry

"Princely" Vendor Bails Out Victoria's Secret

When the Fall 1996 catalog from Victoria's Secret landed in subscribers' mailboxes, order lines immediately lit up. Hundreds of customers had spotted the "faux" shearling coat that was advertised—a tan-colored, suede jacket with fur lining—and couldn't envision going through the upcoming winter without it.

But there was one snag: the coat's supplier, a vendor being used for the first time, began experiencing severe performance problems, says Betsy Hendrickson, Victoria's director of merchandising.

"We had hundreds of the coats on back order, but hadn't received one garment from the supplier by our deadline—it was just one excuse after another," she says. It turns out missed deadlines weren't the vendor's only problem. Once the shipment of coats finally did arrive, they were hardly up to snuff. "They just didn't meet our standards—our customers wouldn't have accepted them—and we couldn't use them," she says. "That was rough, because we had more than 600 people waiting for the coat."

What to do with impatient customers breathing down her neck? Hendrickson quickly got on the phone to another supplier, Sammy Aaron of Marvin Richards Co. Sammy and crew worked overtime to turn around a new order of the coats in under 4 weeks. "Phenomenal, a remarkable feat," she says, given the nature of the coat and the time crunch. "He proved himself a prince among vendors."

Meanwhile, to reassure the increasingly testy customers, Victoria Secret's customer service department helped Hendrickson draft a frank, personal letter explaining reasons for the delay, and delicately asked customers to wait just a bit longer for their garments. "Amazingly, only five customers—fewer than 1%—canceled their orders," she says.

In the end, each coat cost Victoria's Secret about thirty dollars more than planned—not to mention the added aggravation. "But our customers trusted us to deliver, and we honored that trust," Hendrickson says.

Contributed by Mark Ballard

Not to Fear, the Contact Lens Express Is Here

It's every contact wearer's dread: an inadvertent tear of a lens at the most inopportune moment. Sharon Forshee Haukohl was preparing for an important out-of-town journey one morning when, in her haste to get ready, she didn't just tear a lens, but ripped it completely in half.

Haukohl, an executive with an Atlanta-based customer research firm, panicked because she had to get to the airport in a few hours, and she didn't have a back-up pair of glasses. She knew she'd have trouble seeing well enough to drive a car all the way to the airport.

She grabbed a phone book and hastily called America's Best Contacts and Eyeglasses, where she's a member of a contact lens program, and explained her plight to an America's Best associate. To further complicate matters, Sharon had recently moved from Birmingham, AL, to Atlanta, GA, and her lens prescription was still in the Birmingham store. The America's Best associate in Atlanta said she'd do whatever she could to quickly find a pair of contacts Sharon could take on her trip.

Less than 10 minutes later, America's Best was back on the phone to Sharon. They had located the records in Birmingham, and were checking to see if they had her prescription in stock. Lo and behold, the prescription was available, and an associate said Sharon's new contact lens would be waiting for her at the front desk—in under an hour.

"I drove with one eye closed all the way to the store," Haukohl says. "When I arrived, someone immediately approached me and asked me if I was Sharon. It was Jane. She whisked me directly to a register, rang up the new contact lens, and wished me good luck on my trip. I thanked her profusely, rushed to the airport and made my flight with time to spare."

Contributed by Sharon Forshee Haukohl

Trains, Planes, and Automobiles Make This Party Happen

A series of delays had put The TranzAlpine, a scenic passenger train that crosses the Southern Alps in New Zealand, seriously off schedule during an October 1996 run from Greymouth to Christchurch and back. Most of the passengers were none too happy, but one businessman in particular stood out in his frustration. The delays meant he would probably miss the last flight out of Christchurch that evening to his final destination, and he had been away from home for weeks on business. And he knew that his family was going to be awaiting him at the airport with hats, horns, and hugs.

But...Tranz Rail to the rescue. Darin Cusack, a customer service manager with Tranz Scenic, a business unit in the privatized railway, got word of the situation and moved quickly.

He called Hertz to gain access to a second set of keys for the customer's rental car, which was parked back at the railway station in Greymouth.

The on-board train staff arranged for Cusack to meet the customer at a top at an intermediate stop, the Springfield station, about an hour out of Christchurch on the Canterbury Plains. A taxi drove the customer to the outskirts of the city, where Darin had sped to meet him in the rental car, and to hand over the controls. Their deft coordination and quick thinking ensured that the customer was easily able to drive to Christchurch and catch his waiting plane.

Contributed by Tranz Rail Limited, New Zealand

If at First You Don't Succeed, Recover, Recover—and Then Recover Again

Persistence, patience, and pride in one's products are usually the minimum requirements for front-liners looking to satisfy upset customers. Mary Hartke of Lindenwold, NJ, says she ran into a service rep who more than demonstrated those traits.

Hartke was approached at a local retail store by a sales rep of National Studios, a portrait studio headquartered in Missouri. The rep told Hartke about a promotional offer, and Hartke signed up to have her daughter's portrait taken.

But when the final portrait arrived in the mail, Hartke saw that the picture was not properly centered on the background. "As I began writing a letter of complaint," she says, "I couldn't help but feel that my complaint would receive little attention, since I bought only the one promotional portrait."

A representative from National Studios called Hartke after receiving the letter and (surprise, surprise) took immediate responsibility for the complaint. "The rep explained that a problem with the proof caused the difficulty in centering it properly, but offered to have the studio do the best it could to correct the problem," says Hartke. "Then she told me she'd have the new portrait sent to her attention first, so she could ensure its quality before mailing it on to my home."

The same representative called after previewing the second attempt and said that while the new portrait was better than the original, she still felt Hartke wouldn't be completely satisfied with it. The rep said she'd mail Hartke the portrait—but then offered another alternative in order to fix the problem. The portrait, she said, could be redone on a plain background without the overlay, thus eliminating the centering problem. Hartke agreed.

The customer was more than pleased with the end result—and just a little bit stunned. "I've now received a total of three portraits from this company, at no extra charge whatsoever, and I am totally satisfied with my finished product," Hartke says.

A Premature Reservation and a
Mind-Blowing Redemption

It was a foggy January night in San Ramon, CA, and Jim Clepper was having trouble locating his hotel. Just as he was about to give up, he came upon a sign that read "Marriott construction gate."

Through a computer glitch at Marriott Hotels and Resorts' reservation center, Clepper had been booked at a Marriott that wasn't slated to open for 6 months.

Although a bit agitated, Clepper wasn't overly perturbed about the incident; he found a room in a nearby town and went about his business. But his travel agent suggested he write a note of complaint to the hotel chairman, J.W. Marriott. He did, and the result made Clepper a Marriott fan for life.

Marriott sent him a personal letter of apology along with a voucher for a free night's stay. "I thought that was the end of it," says Clepper. It was more like the beginning. Soon after, Marriott's reservations department also wrote to apologize. "Then I thought it was over for sure," he says.

Not so. The matter came to the attention of a marketing director at the new Marriott in San Ramon, who told general manager Ron Cribbet about the incident. The two decided to have some fun with it. Clepper would be brought back when the hotel was open for some better business treatment.

The welcome mat included free first-class air travel from Houston to Oakland. At Oakland International Airport, a helicopter picked up Clepper and his wife and flew them to the hotel's front door, where all the employees were standing and waving in greeting.

3
Savoring Those "Daily Delights"

Little things mean a lot. The coffee shop waitress who smiles and calls you by name when you come through the door. The druggist who takes a few seconds out to acknowledge your youngster. The video store clerk who comes out from behind the counter to help you find a movie he just knows you're going to enjoy. The grocery store meat man who remembers to ask how you enjoyed the chops you bought last week.

Little things.

In the business school journals, the professors use terms like "value-adding behavior" and "pursuing an intimacy strategy." But beyond that stiff and sterile language, customer service, done right, is simply people helping people get through the day with a little dignity and a little joy. Human beings helping one another get their needs met, and taking the time to do the little things that make the process civil and comfortable, enjoyable and positive. It is waitresses and barbers and delivery people and butchers and telephone operators and civil servants and doctors and dentists who care enough to take the time to remember that customers are people like themselves; people with hopes and fears, confusions and problems and temperaments, egos and needs—and questions.

The stories in this chapter aren't about rescues at sea or marshaling helicopters to make delivery deadlines or of saving customers thousands of dollars or hundreds of hours of time. They are, rather, stories of the little things that someone did for someone else. Stories of small kindness' extended—and remembered fondly. In many of them, the teller adds something about the economic impact of the kindness, some form of: "And I've shopped there at Mary's store ever since," or "And now I won't let anyone but Roger work on my car." And that's important, that obvious economic benefit. But equally important is the feeling that the Sams and Cynthias who told the stories about the Marys and Rogers have been a part of a small civilizing experience with another human being.

In today's hectic, break-neck paced world, that is, ironically, much more than a "little thing."

Amazing Roger's Auto Body Shop Breaks the Mold

My friend Lindsay Willis is one of those super charged, over achieving, fast talking, fast thinking people who, for all that energy, is always fun to sit and talk with—or just listen to. There is always something interesting going on in her life.

And why wouldn't there be? Lindsay is a premiere customer service researcher, a lay minister in the Speak of the Word Church, an avid golfer with a shamefully low handicap, and, if truth be known, a little bit of a hot rodder. She's not a bad or dangerous driver—she just needs to be places in a hurry. So she does. Hurry, that is.

So I wasn't totally surprised when she reported that her shiny new gold Mercedes had been in an accident—though, admittedly, it wasn't an accident of her causing. What was surprising was the memorable service Lindsay received at the hands of Roger's Body Shop in Minneapolis, MN.

Roger's wowed her from minute one. The establishment, she noted, was clean, almost to the point of being spotless. And no more than 3 minutes after she walked through the front door, an estimator was at work—assessing the extent of the damage to her rear bumper, a process that took less than 15 minutes. Oh, and while the estimator was looking her car over, he called a car rental agency to see what sort of deal he could get on a rental while her car was being worked on. "I don't want to put you in an Escort for the week it's going to take to repair your car, " he told her, and continued to call around in search of a car closer to her obvious personal preferences.

Any question that she booked the repair with Roger's?

But that's just the overture. A day later Lindsay received a card in the mail reminding her of the day she was to bring the car back for the repairs, and that the repair would indeed take a week, but that the rental car would be ready when she brought

her car back. And the repair did indeed take 5 days—just as promised. During that time, she received two calls updating her on the status of the work. The first call informed her that the other driver's insurance company adjuster had been in to look at the car, and that Roger's was about to order a part needed for the repair. The second call was to inform her that the part was in, and that the repair would be finished on schedule.

When she arrived, Lindsay noted that not only had the repair been done perfectly, but her car had also been washed, vacuumed, and the floor mats cleaned. A week after she picked up the car, she received this follow-up call, "Hi. This is Marv from Roger's Auto Body. We just wanted to know if everything was great with your car, and with our repair process (it was). If anything comes up, feel free to call me personally and we'll take care of it immediately."

Automobile dealers, used car salespeople, and auto repair shops are almost always at the bottom of the pile in customer satisfaction surveys and esteem—usually just above politicians and cable television companies. But as Lindsay Willis's experience amply proves, that certainly isn't a part of the natural order of the universe, just the way some have come to let their businesses be run.

Ron Zemke

A Ritzy Greeting Wows Spouse—and Brings This Couple Back Again and Again

Those little things that mean a lot have created a strong bond between that colleague of ours you've met before, Chip Bell, his wife Nancy, and the Ritz-Carlton hotel chain. The Bells had been apart on business for two long weeks—she in Washington D.C., he in Charlotte and Dallas. To make up for the separation and put a little pampering in their reunion, they decided to rendezvous in Atlanta and spend a long weekend at the sumptuous Ritz-Carlton Buckhead. Their affection for this Ritz-Carlton was cemented forever when the hotel doorman conspired with Chip to greet Nancy in the hotel's driveway—with her favorite drink on a silver tray.

"Dr. Bell," the doorman told her soothingly when she pulled up at the hotel's front door, "I believe you've been looking forward to this. Just leave your keys in the ignition, and let us take care of everything for you. Please have a wonderful weekend." Needless to say, the Bells remember the weekend, the Ritz-Carlton Buckhead, and that doorman very fondly. And they've been back many times since.

Kristin Anderson

Kid's Meal for the Big Guy

Richard DeBurgh, chairman of the Child Nutrition Research Committee of the California Association of School Officials, had phoned Meg Fleig, a counterpart with the Corona Norco Unified School District, with a request. Seems Mr. DeBurgh and five of his fellow committee members would be flying into an airport near Meg's location for a meeting, and were looking for a conference room and lunch for six, at no cost!

Meg readily agreed to help out. When the committee arrived, they found their meeting room prepped and ready to go, with coffee, fresh fruit, and sweet rolls available—none of which had been requested by the group.

At lunch time, as five meticulously prepared deluxe salads were rolled out, Mr. DeBurgh told the staff he would prefer not to have salad. "No problem," said a staff member, smiling. "We have a special meal for you." She went back into the kitchen and brought out a Taco Bell children's meal with three toys.

Seems Meg had contacted each of the districts after receiving the initial phone call, found out what the favored meal of each committee member was, and had tracked down and prepared their favorite luncheon meals in advance—without the committee knowing!

Contributed by Tami Cline

Salting Away a Snowbound Customer's Pain

A customer called the Ace Hardware store in Friday Harbor, WA, an island off that state's coast, in a state of panic. A rare, late spring snowstorm had boxed him in and threatened to cost him an important meeting back on the mainland. The man couldn't get out of his driveway due to the slippery incline, and desperately needed to catch the morning ferry—a very large order hung on his ability to make the meeting. Trapped in the driveway, he had called an Ace store hoping for a delivery of sidewalk salt. Ace employee Gerry Larson took the call, assuring the customer someone would get out to him right away.

Sure enough, David Hayworth drove out to the customer's home through the accumulating snow, and not only delivered the salt, but applied it to the entire driveway so the customer could make a hasty escape and catch the boat to the mainland.

The customer was so grateful that when he returned that evening, he not only sent back a long thank-you note, but attached it to a gift of assorted gourmet jelly beans for David.

Contributed by JoAnn Mueller

"Good Samaritan" Travel Agency Eases Pain of Passenger with Dying Mother

A Denver woman dashed into Professional Travel Corporation's (PTC) office on opening day at the Denver International Airport, unable to hold back the tears. It was 10 A.M.

Forty minutes earlier the woman's sister had called and delivered the sad news that their mother was dying in a Milwaukee hospital. By 10:10 A.M. the woman was nervously explaining to one of PTC's travel agents that her flight had a connection in Chicago, and she was very afraid she wouldn't get to Milwaukee in time.

Robyn Zimmermann, manager of Professional Travel's DIA's office, understood the customer's worry and moved swiftly to help. She wrote a new ticket for a direct flight into Milwaukee that left in just 12 minutes. Jerri Wheelhouse, another PTC agent, then rushed to Concourse B to hold up the United Airlines flight as Robyn put the finishing touches on the ticket.

Professional Travel vice president Margie Grimes ran with the client to the airport train and to Gate B-50, where she made her flight.

"It was such a neat way for us to start off our new office at the airport," Margie said.

Contributed by Robyn Zimmermann

For the Colorado Rockies, Service Is Part of Their Game

For the 3.4 million baseball fans who attended one of the Colorado Rockies 81 home games last year, hits, runs, and errors— along with a helping or two of peanuts, popcorn, and Cracker Jacks—were probably the measure of a good day. But for the five groups that work together to provide customer service at every Rockies home game at Denver's Coors Field, a good day at the ballpark is measured as much by the number of lost little leaguers united with parents, valuables returned to their rightful owners, and special requests responded to, as it is by the box score of the game.

Nicole Jacobsen, manager of Coors Field Relations, is extremely proud of the 2,000 guest services reps—most of whom are part time, seasonal employees—and the special care they take of Colorado Rockies fans during each home game. Even more impressive is the fact that only a small percentage of the Coors Field Guest Services Staff are actually Colorado Rockies employees. Most are employees of Colorado Rockies partnering companies that manage the field security, parking, maintenance, ticket taking, ushering, and concession responsibilities. Nicole has every reason to be proud. Last year Coors Field reunited more than 50% of their lost articles with the people who misplaced them—more than 1,500 pieces. The remainder are sent to the Denver Police Department for possible claiming after the season. Additionally, the Rockies receive roughly 150 comment cards per game, which translates into about 12,450 for the season. Some of these comments are obviously requests for seat repair, or missing cup holders, but of those 150, just about 40 each game receive a personal response from a member of the stadium services department. That translates to about 3,320 each season.

What does great service look like at Coors Field? It looks like Brian S. who spent an hour and a half after a Rockies game walking the surrounding neighborhood with a six-year-old child who had become separated from his older brother and couldn't remember his address. The boys had walked the 12 blocks from home to the game. And great service looks like Kelly G., who pushed a fan the fourteen blocks from the park to his home when the battery on his electric wheelchair went dead.

Distance doesn't seem to be a barrier to service for members of the Rockies guest relations team. When an elderly couple missed the charter bus from the ballpark back to their home in Greely, CO, 54 miles from Denver, Mark D. simply loaded them and their wheelchairs into his van and drove them home. Not to be outdone, Stacy S., another Rockie's service team member, drove a family of four home to Ft. Collins, an hour and a half away, when they became separated from their car keys.

Taking care of customers sometimes extends beyond the members of the guest services team to the ballplayers themselves. During the 1996 season, a guest was hit by a foul ball off the bat of outfielder Dante Bichette. The next day Bichette visited the guest at her home—and ended up staying for dinner.

By the way, if you're ever at Coors Field and in need of a guest relations person, they're easy to find—they are, quite literally, the ones in the white hats.

Contributed by Nicole Jacobsen

GE Answer Center Cooks Up a Big One

The GE Answer Center in Louisville, KY, knows all about tough calls. Calls are automatically routed so that representatives receive 100 calls a day, 10,000 to 15,000 a week, and 3 million a year. On average, a representative spends almost 4 minutes with each customer. They get about 90 seconds in between calls. Customers generally call in to ask about their GE appliances or where they can purchase a part or find out how to fix something. Occasionally, however, more interesting requests are at the other end of the line.

Nothing exemplifies the center's motto—"One Team...Better and Faster Than Anybody Else in the World"—more clearly than the actions of Marsha White, a center rep, who usually does whatever it takes to satisfy customers—even if it means sharing her own personal belongings with essential strangers.

A GE customer called Marsha looking for one of GE's famed *Microwave Guide and Cookbooks* —except she wanted a version first published in the early 1980s, a version that has been updated several times since. "I tried to interest her in one of our new cookbooks, but she really had her heart set on that old one, and the recipes in it," Marsha says. "When she described the book's cover, I realized it was one I had in my own cookbook collection. She offered to buy it from me, but I told her that every cookbook deserves to be used, and I'd be glad to send it to her free, since she would use it."

Here's the letter the customer sent to GE's CEO Jack Welch following the episode.

Dear Mr. Welch:

I have been looking for one of your older *Microwave Guide and Cookbooks* for some time. I was unable to locate one so I called the General Electric Co. to see if you had one on a back shelf somewhere. I talked with Marsha White (of the GE Answer Center). Marsha said that you didn't have anymore cookbooks, but that she had one at home—her own—she would share with me. Marsha talked with her supervisor, Tina Hammons, and they agreed to send it to me.

Now, I think that's beyond the call of duty.

We built a new home and have all GE appliances in it. I know you have a lot of good employees, but in my book Marsha White and Tina Hammons are GREAT!

Sincerely,

Nelta Rea

Contributed by Merrell Grant

These Delivery Men Cometh—and Serve Up Delight

Go ahead, count how many times you've had a delivery service, whether its cargo be refrigerators, pianos, or furniture, either fail to show up at the appointed hour, or demonstrate an alarming lack of concern or imagination in trying to squeeze your bed or sofa through the front door.

Okay, now put your calculator down.

Even once is too much, believe the managers of Merchants Home Delivery Service, which makes some 4 million deliveries to consumers' homes in North America every year for the likes of Levitz, Sears, and Circuit City. The company works hard to counter the oft-tarnished image of delivery services. Case in point, this glowing letter from a customer who praised two delivery men who work for Levitz Furniture in Westboro, MA, part of the Merchant's delivery chain.

To:

Merchants Home Delivery System

I just had to let you know about the delivery team of Bill and Mike Leland, the two great guys who showed up to deliver my new sofa and chair. They were pleasant, courteous, and totally professional. When the sofa I ordered wouldn't fit through my doorway—even though the salesman in the store had assured me it would, never mind that I supplied him with exact measurements to my apartment's entryway—Bill and Mike made it their business to find another way to complete their delivery.

A few months ago I had ordered a sofa and chair from one of your competitors, and when the sofa would not fit through my doorway, the delivery men told me they could not deliver it through the window. It just couldn't be done, they said. Then, reconsidering, they said they'd do it for $200 cash. I ended up giving everything back and went shopping at Levitz instead. In the meantime, I had no living room furniture for 8 weeks, and had to use lounge chairs.

But when Bill and Mike from Levitz, (Levitz deliveries are done by Merchants), still could not make it fit through the door, they began looking for another solution to the problem. And they never asked for a thing! Their only concern was to complete the delivery. Finally, they got it in through a window.

You are to be congratulated for selecting these two individuals to be part of the Levitz team. Because of them, I will continue to shop at Levitz and spread the word to my family and friends about the positive experience I had there.

Signed,

A grateful customer

Contributed by Ken Barry

Taking a "Chicken Lickin'" and Still Tickin'

Tony Iyoob, a training specialist with Harris Teeter Inc. grocery stores, handled an irate customer in a way that offers a lesson in self-control for us all.

An angry customer had returned a spoiled chicken to Tony's store. The problem: it was one of his competitor's chickens." But the customer proceeded to tell me how slack our store was in selling spoiled meat, and wouldn't let me get a word in edgewise," Tony says. "The yelling didn't let up for a second."

Tony let her finish venting, and when she finished he apologized, letting her know his company cared about her concerns. He then gently pointed out her chicken was purchased from a competitor, but that he would be happy to replace it with one of his own. "She was mortified and felt bad about giving me such a hard time," he says. "I insisted she let me replace the chicken, but she refused. She then left the store."

About an hour later, Tony noticed her shopping in his produce department, and when she saw him she ran up and gave another heartfelt apology. She went on to explain the reason she was there was, "If you can back up a product from another chain as well as you did, then I can only imagine how you would back up one of your own products." She said she was committed to doing any future shopping in Tony's store, and he's indeed seen her several times since the day of the infamous "Chicken Lickin"—she gave him.

Retail Redress

Marsha Blackwell was thrilled with the new dress she had found at a Parisian department store in Birmingham, AL. "Perfect for my class reunion," she thought. Except for the sleeves, which needed shortening. She asked Parisian's alterations department if it could pin the sleeves. No problem, they said.

But when Marsha returned to pick up the dress the night before the reunion, Parisian service workers found it had mistakenly been placed in the Ladies' Ready-to-Wear Department, and the sleeves had not yet been altered.

A store manager, made aware of the problem after the dress was found, offered to do the alterations on the spot—it was nearly an hour beyond store closing—but Blackwell had other pressing business, and said it would be more convenient for her to return the next morning.

At 9 A.M. the next day, the sleeves were fitted and altered to perfection. In addition, Parisian gave Blackwell a 25% discount off the dress price, waived alteration charges, and the manager apologized for the inconvenience with a box of chocolate-chip cookies from a nearby cookie shop.

Says Blackwell, "They made me feel like I was the most important customer at Parisian. I remember their kindness and concern each time I go shopping."

Pampered Limo Passengers Avoid Being Smothered by Samsonite

John Bailey of Bailey Travel in York, PA, had booked a family from nearby Spring Grove a dream luxury vacation. The family of six would cruise from New York to London on the QE2, explore Picadilly Circus, Big Ben and other sights, and then dash back home aboard the Concorde. Everything went smoothly and as planned until the family returned to New York.

On the trip from Pennsylvania to New York to pick up the family on its return, the travel agency's limo driver called John Bailey, head of the travel firm, to tell him luggage space looked tight, and he was concerned about room for the family on the trip home. With extra packages from the shopping excursion the family had planned in New York, they'd likely have to hold the luggage in their laps on the 200-mile ride from Kennedy Airport to Spring Grove.

So the travel firm lived up to its "exceeding expectations" corporate motto: Mr. Bailey immediately called to send another driver and his own car to carry just the client's luggage, so they could travel home in comfort, with plenty of leg room to spare.

The thoughtfulness resulted not only in a handsome tip for the limo driver, but for Mr. Bailey as well—the first he's ever received as head of the agency, he says.

Contributed by John Bailey

"People Over Paperwork" Philosophy Is Its Own Reward

It was a routine phone call. A policyholder from Northwestern Mutual Life (NML) Insurance Co. wanted to know how much she could borrow on her life insurance policies, and what effect the loan would have on her insurance protection. Wendy Goetz, a Northwestern Mutual customer relations rep, promised to call her back with all the details at a convenient time. The policyholder said anytime would be convenient, since she was disabled and largely house-bound. Wendy immediately asked how long she'd been disabled. "Since 1986," the policyholder said.

Wendy quickly checked all of the woman's life insurance policies and discovered one had a benefit under which she didn't have to pay premiums if she became totally disabled. The policyholder had overlooked this benefit and had been paying the premiums anyway.

When Wendy told her she would be receiving a refund of 10 years worth of premiums, her response was a heartfelt "God Bless You."

Wendy isn't the only NML employee who puts customers high on her agenda.

Another policyholder visiting Milwaukee stopped in at Northwestern Mutual headquarters—without an appointment—to make some changes to his insurance. David Radl responded and dropped his other work to help the customer, and called in Jody Bauer for extra assistance. The duo spent 2 hours with the customer, helping him transfer his policies into a trust. Jody answered his questions, and prepared and input all the necessary forms on the spot.

The policyholder was so delighted with David and Jody's attention and solution to his unsolvable problem that he decided to transfer the other 90% of his life insurance, which had been with another company, to Northwestern Mutual's trusted hands.

Contributed by Carol Haiar

St. Luke's Medical Center's Fan Mail Says It All

No one has to tell the employees of St. Luke's Medical Center in Milwaukee, WI, that patients are people, too. In a health care industry increasingly obsessed with cost containment, occupied beds, and squeezing more from the bottom line, that's no small accomplishment. Particularly when you couple it with the fact hospitals are naturally places few want to enter, and plenty are anxious to leave.

But St. Luke's, with its internal "Golden Sneaker" award for service excellence fueling the action, continues to stand out as safe haven for those looking for more than a "cattle-drive" hospital experience. The focus on patient needs isn't an aberration, mind you, but one carried out with work-a-day consistency.

Just ask the Center's growing legions of patient-fans, who've penned these letters of thanks to memorable employees they've encountered.

To: St. Luke's Medical Center

I am writing this letter about someone special at St. Luke's. His name is Mike Laven. He is the man who parks the cars for the valet service. In the last two and a half years, he has parked our truck at least 100 times. My husband has been fighting cancer and St. Luke's has been our second home. When my husband was in the hospital, I would wait for a ride home each day. Mike always asked about my husband. Many times he told me to make sure I ate well and got enough rest. He knew by looking at me that I cried more than I slept or ate.

And then came the day I saw Mike crying. I found out he had just lost someone to cancer a few hours before. That's when I realized just how special he was. Always smiling, always caring—even when his own heart was heavy. In October, we saw Mike for the first time in six months. My husband is in remission, and Mike has shared our happiness. When we drove up in our white truck, his smile was there, but I also saw a hit of concern in his face that made me say, "We're just here for a check up" to assure him. Mike's smile grew.

Many times I have walked into that hospital with my heart a little higher. Why? Because of a man who can make the day better with his smile.

Sincerely,

Mildred James

To: St. Luke's Medical Center

After having heart bypass surgery, I was a very sick man. This lady, this wonderful lady (St. Luke's nursing assistant Cindy Pastick), treated me with such kindness I will never forget it. I was here from Boston all by myself, and I asked her to sit with me a while because I was so sick and scared. I was having trouble breathing.

She sat and held my hand until I fell asleep, staying almost an hour after she was scheduled to go home. Then, she noticed that someone had rolled my clothes up into a ball, so she took them home and washed and ironed them so I would look halfway decent when I caught my plane home to Boston.

Believe me, I will remember that kindness for the rest of my life.

Sincerely,

Mark Lewis

Here's yet one more story illustrating how St. Luke's sets itself apart from the hospital masses.

A St. Luke's orthopedic patient lost an inexpensive but favorite pair of sneakers during a long stay at the hospital. Housekeeping, after learning of the man's complaint, concluded that someone had mistakenly thrown out the sneakers, and was quick to offer a heartfelt apology.

Not good enough; offers to pay for the patient's sneakers were also not satisfactory. The patient, who wanted his sneakers for physical therapy, was being discharged the next day and wanted *those* sneakers back.

The traditional response at that point would likely have been a diplomatically insipid form letter along the lines of, "Thank you for bringing this matter to our attention. Your satisfaction is our only goal. If we can ever..." end of story. Instead, two housekeepers who had taken some phone calls during the incident took over. Acting on their own, and not on managerial directive, they got a detailed description of the sneakers from the patient, left work, went to a store and—using their own money—purchased a replacement pair of identical sneakers.

The patient was surprised—and elated. The two housekeepers received St. Luke's first-ever award for a most meritorious act of empowerment, called none other than the aforementioned Golden Sneaker Award.

Contributed by Allen Stasiewski

His Name Was Freddie

An employee at the Inn at the Park Hotel in Anaheim, CA—known to us only as Freddie—went beyond service excellence to give a customer something even more rare and valuable: personal trust.

Freddie, a registration desk attendant, was approached by a hotel guest who had lost her watch at the swimming pool. She asked if anyone had turned in a watch matching her description. Freddie checked and said no watches had been found, but assured her he would let her know if that changed.

Realizing that the guest might have some trouble keeping her appointments for the day without a timepiece, Freddie offered to lend her his own until hers turned up, or until she could replace it. She accepted his generous offer.

The customer's watch was never found. But Freddie's friendly concern and willingness to trust a guest turned what could've been remembered as a bad day into a surprisingly delightful one.

Small Kindnesses Enrich Both Giver and Receiver

Juana Ardon-de-Lemus was feeling a little sorry for herself for drawing the Christmas day shift at the Sheraton Seattle Hotel & Towers, taking her away from her husband and small children on this cherished holiday. But her personal disappointment seemed small when she encountered a guest who was stranded there in Seattle, cut off from friends and family back home, and holed up alone and unhappy in her room. Juana, a room attendant, chatted with the unhappy woman as she made up the room, freshened the towels, and generally went about her duties.

When she finished comforting the woman, Juana went directly back to that floor's staging area and called the front desk to report the guest's plight. In no time, a bottle of wine and a box of chocolates, along with a note of Christmas cheer, was delivered to the woman's room. And Juana finished her own lonely shift feeling very much a part of the true Christmas spirit.

Contributed by Mary Wieth

Giving a Young Bone Marrow Patient a Crucial Lifeline to the Outside World

Life saving miracle though it is, the prospect of a bone marrow transplant—a high-tech, some say still-experimental, cancer treatment—can be both a frightening and lonely experience, as a seventeen-year-old boy found out while awaiting the procedure at Oregon Health Sciences University Hospital (OHSU).

Nancy Boyle, a social worker at OHSU, learned from chatting with the boy that he was an avid computer hacker, and that he greatly missed being able to communicate with his schoolmates and school by computer while in the hospital. He wondered if the hospital could set up a temporary e-mail address for him on its computer system.

Nancy quickly got in touch with Kathi Lauder in the information technology department to see if this could be done for a nonemployee. Kathi said it'd be a first for the hospital, but pushed forward. With a minimum of discussion she was given an enthusiastic green light, and soon the boy was back in touch with his friends and school on a daily basis, from the comfort of a computer terminal in his own room.

Contributed by Patricia Southard

Andersonville or Bust

One doesn't usually equate warm and toasty service with the National Park Service, but Jim Dehlman, a New York visitor to a historic site in Georgia, found a healthy Southern-fried helping of it.

Dehlman had flown to Atlanta for a short visit with his brother, and the two had scheduled a drive south of the city to visit the historic site at Andersonville, an old Civil War stockade and cemetery.

Due to some engine trouble, the brothers didn't arrive at the site until 5:25 P.M.—only to discover a "Park closed at 5:30" sign. "Needless to say, I was highly disappointed because it would be one of my few chances to see the site," says Dehlman. "But then I noticed someone come out of the Administration Building and drive to the entrance station. The gate was still partially open so I walked up to the building and knocked on the door."

Ranger Alan Marsh answered the door, and, after hearing the brothers' story, invited them to drive into the park—even with a pontoon boat in tow—to tour the facility, and take their sweet time in doing so.

Says Dehlman, "When we finished, he met up with us again, told us a little more about Andersonville, answered all of our questions, and then showed us the graves of the six renegades that we had been unable to find. All of this after closing hours, on what I'm sure was his own time. All in all, the courtesy, hospitality, and compassion he showed us was amazing."

Contributed by John Quinley

Customer Service Is not a Mickey Mouse Affair

Valerie Oberle, a vice president with Disney University's Guest Program in Orlando, relates a story to *Chicken Soup for the Soul at Work* that shows exactly how Walt Disney's renowned service ethic looks in practice.

"Not too long ago, a guest checking out of our Polynesian Village Resort at Walt Disney World was asked how she enjoyed her visit. She told the front-desk clerk she had had a wonderful vacation, but was heartbroken about losing several rolls of Kodacolor film she had not yet developed. She was particularly upset over the loss of the pictures she had shot at our Polynesian Luau, a memory she especially treasured.

"Now, understand Disney has no written service standards concerning lost luau snapshots. Fortunately, the hostess at the front desk understood Disney's philosophy of caring for our guests. She asked the woman to leave her a couple of rolls of fresh film, promising she would take care of the rest.

"Two weeks later, the guest received a package at home. In it were photos of the entire cast of our luau show, personally autographed by each performer. There were also photos of the Disney parade and fireworks from the theme park, taken by the front-desk hostess on her own time, after work. I happen to know this story because the guest wrote us a letter. She said she had never received such compassionate service from a business establishment.

"Heroic service does not come from policy manuals. It comes from people who care."

Contributed by Valerie Oberle

4

Service From the Heart

"To serve," in the commercial marketplace sense of the verb, conjures images of buyer-seller, boss-subordinate, demands, wants, needs, expectations, and compliance. There must be a thousand maxims that exhort organizations—and individuals—

to be mindful of service if they are to be financially successful. To wit:

> Put service and quality first. The money will take care of itself.

> Live by this ironclad rule: All promises to customers are kept. PERIOD.

> Sales Creates Customers. Service Keeps Them.

"To serve" has also a richer, more profound meaning and connotation. The service of a pastor to a congregation. The devotion of child to an aging parent. The commitment of an individual to a higher cause. These too are service.

"Service from the heart" is that place, that intersection of the corporate and humanitarian meanings of service in the workplace. It is that place, those incidents, those times when caring individuals—and organizations as a composite of caring people, perhaps as a community—take action. And do things for others that, yes, are an expression of an organization, but are really at their core an extension of human selflessness from one person—or two or three—for the simple benefit of others.

In its simplest form, "service from the heart" is empathy; a display of understanding for a customer, colleague, or fellow human. It's a message that says, "I understand and I appreciate." But most often, service from the heart is about actions. Going out of the way to make another person's life better, easier, more whole.

It is the extending of oneself, and even the resources of the organization, beyond the narrow logical strictures of "return-on-investment" and "long-term retention probability." It is deeds done in service to a need that no civilized person would feel good about leaving unmet.

The Gospel According to Nordstrom

For most organizations, customer service is a strategic tool and tactical weapon, a tool to foster customer loyalty and repeat business. The bottom line is the preeminent focus. Fair enough.

But in a select few other organizations, there's another dimension, where customer care is a fetish, a point of pride, a leading part of the corporate message, culture, and myths. Where customer service is delivered as much from the heart as the head, out of an authentic desire to make the lives of fellow humans a bit brighter, even for a select few minutes or hours.

One of the most consistent and long-time exemplars of that obsession is Seattle-based retailer Nordstrom Inc. The stories about dazzled customers are legend. Beneath those stories is a simple dignity and respect for customers.

Nowhere is that message better told than in the introduction to *Fabled Service: Ordinary Acts, Extraordinary Outcomes* (Pfieffer & Co, 1995) by Betsy Sanders, who formerly led Nordstrom's billion dollar Southern California division.

"The congregation sat hushed, unusually attentive even for a church in which they were accustomed to hearing powerful preaching. There had been speculation all week due to the sign in front of the church that proclaimed a sermon with the unlikely theme of *The Gospel According to Nordstrom*. Although members of the prosperous flock were no strangers to Nordstrom in their neighborhood, they couldn't imagine what this mecca of merchandising had to do with Gospel principles.

"The homilist, Rev. Carolyn Crawford, skillfully evoked the luxurious and bustling atmosphere of a Nordstrom store during the holidays...the sights of abundant decorations, the sounds of holiday music expertly performed by an elegantly tuxedoed piano player...the crowds of shoppers laden with parcels. This shared reverie was jarred, however, when Rev. Crawford introduced an improbable character to the scene—a bag lady in torn, filthy clothes.

"Convinced this visitor's presence would be as unwelcome as it was incongruous, Rev. Crawford followed the bag lady through the store with the intent of intervening with security and softening the blow to the woman's dignity when she was asked to leave. The Reverend's original interest in this visitor, who presented such a stark contrast to the gracious abundance of the store, changed to incredulity. No one attempted to stop the bag lady as she entered the elegant and pricey Special Occasions Department. Instead, she was greeted warmly by a smartly attired saleswoman.

"Rev. Crawford, eavesdropping from the adjoining fitting room, was astonished at the salesperson's solicitous responses to the customer. When the customer asked to try on evening dresses, the salesperson brought in gown after gown. With infinite patience, the salesperson evaluated which were the most flattering and appropriate. When the bag lady left the fitting room, her head was held high and there was a light in her eye. She had been treated like a valuable human being.

"When questioned about her actions by Rev. Crawford, the Nordstrom saleswoman replied, "This is what we are here for: To serve and to be kind." Rev. Crawford was moved by this act of dignity exhibited in, of all places, a department store. In addressing her congregation, she asked, "Could we say the same thing about ourselves as church goers? That we're here to serve and to be kind?"

The sermon's message spread far beyond the walls of the church that Sunday morning. The congregation carried the story to friends and associates, and *The New York Times* highlighted the incident. Demand for the sermon was so great that the church eventually sold audiotape copies; employees in Southern California's Nordstrom stores were both humbled and challenged as they listened to the tape. Everyone agreed the incident represented Nordstrom at its best. The story raised not only customer expectations, but also the store personnel's self expectations. In a culture that asked employees to give their best to customers under all circumstances, the definition of best had just been raised."

Ron Zemke

Full Fare Service at a Discount Store

Target Stores, a discount store chain owned by Dayton Hudson Corp., is fast developing a reputation for customer care and above-and-beyond service to customers. The following pair of incidents, offered by Pat Daniels, the company's guest relations administrator show just how far the "above and beyond" value extends for Target associates.

On May 24, 1996, Carol McDowell was shopping in a Target store in Elgin, IL. She was yet again in search of a pair of what were proving to be very elusive "Superman" pajamas for her six-year-old son, Jon-Paul. They had been looking for these particular pajamas for years, but without much luck. To Jon-Paul's absolute delight, Mom was able to find the pajamas at Target that day, a pair very much like those Jon-Paul had worn when he was two and had pined to have replaced in a size suitable for a six-year-old.

But the mood quickly soured when they discovered that none of the pajamas in the store were in Jon-Paul's size. Mom and son were about to give up when Target employee Tina Taylor showed up and asked how she could help. Carol explained the predicament, with more than a little help from Jon-Paul, who by that point had tears welling in his eyes.

Tina called the Target store in nearby West Dundee, but they too were out of stock in Jon-Paul's size. The boy was crushed. But Tina didn't stop there. She called another store, this one in Schaumburg, which—lo and behold—did indeed have some large-size Superman pajamas available, and promised to ship them to the Elgin store. Carol and Jon-Paul went home to wait for Tina's call that the PJ's were in. "When I arrived to pick them up, I found out that Tina had driven all the way to Schaumburg, 15 miles away, paid for the pajamas out of her own pocket, and brought them back to the Elgin store just for us," Carol says, adding, "My son and I thanked her profusely. Tina's response? `That's how we do things here at Target; I'm glad we could help.' Most employees would take the personal credit, not pass it over to their company. I haven't seen this kind of service in years."

Becky McIntire of Iowa was so impressed with service she received at Target that the experience stayed close to her heart for over a year, culminating in a letter to Target guest relations administrator, Pat Daniels, which we've excerpted below.

I know this is very late in coming but this whole past year it has not left my mind for long that I owe you a great deal of thanks! You not only found us Power Ranger toys for our son, Craig, but you wrapped them and mailed them to us at no charge! You did so much to make Craig's Christmas of 1993 a most special one! Those Power Ranger toys, as you well know, were in such high demand, but in so low supply. Craig had already been through so much that year since June with chemotherapy and all that goes with it. It would have been so difficult to explain to him that Santa didn't have any Power Ranger toys for him. With your most generous help we didn't have to do that! I just want you to know how much we appreciate your thoughtfulness, and that as a Target employee you and your company have extended much good will.

I thought you might be interested to know that Craig's chemotherapy ended January 31, 1994 and he continued in remission until June 4th. Then he had more chemotherapy and was a candidate for a bone marrow transplant. He had that on August 4, 1994. After a 7-week hospital stay he was released on September 12, 1994 and has had weekly follow up with the BMT clinic ever since. So far he is doing okay. He is still a Power Ranger maniac. Ha! Those toys, thank goodness, became in greater supply during 1994 so we didn't have to go "begging" and searching this past Christmas time as we did in 1993. I am so thankful for that!

I will enclose our Christmas letters from 1993 and 1994, since it gives a much better look at Craig's life than I could put in this notecard. I just thought you'd like to know more about the boy you and Target helped to be very happy last Christmas.

We've been blessed to have Craig and all six of us together this Christmas again. Though we live with the knowledge that our lives can change in a matter of moments.

Again, please know how much we appreciate and thank you for your Power Ranger toys for Christmas 1993 for Craig. (By the way—I LOVE to shop at Target!)

Sincerely,

The McIntires

Contributed by Pat Daniels

Nursing Homes with Heart

Beverly Health and Rehabilitation Services, Inc., is part of Arkansas-based Beverly Enterprises, the largest provider of nursing home, rehabilitation, and hospice services in the United States. The forsworn goal of Beverly Health's employees, the nursing home part of the company, is to create "Magical Moments" for residents; the kind of cherished experiences and memories that enliven their days—and are still talked about and recounted weeks or months later.

Squire McCain, a resident at Starmount Health and Rehabilitation Center in Greensboro, NC, had a dream: To meet talk-show host Oprah Winfrey. Knowing the odds against getting show tickets—and the unlikelihood of his ever being able to afford the trip to Chicago where the show originates—Squire never seriously expected his dream to come true.

But it wasn't an impossible dream to some employees at the center. Tammy Todd, a social worker, and Rick Woodrum, a nursing supervisor, quietly made a pact to make Squire's dream come true.

After numerous false starts and dead ends, Tammy finally made contact with the Oprah show's audience coordinator. Impressed by Tammy and Rick's determination, she not only came up with seat reservations for a show, but took care of booking the airline and hotel accommodations as well.

But how would they fund the incidentals and expenses of the trip? "Thanks to the kind hearts of other Starmount associates, visitors, and friends, we raised nearly $500—and that's before the serious fund raising began," says Woodrum.

Once the big day arrived, Squire—accompanied by three center employees—left Starmount in a limousine, with a local Greensboro news channel there to see him off. When they arrived at Chicago's O'Hare airport later that morning, they were met by a Lincoln Town Car and driven to the Tremont Hotel.

Early the next morning, the group was driven to Harpo Studios in another white, stretch limousine. Squire and the group received VIP treatment at the show, including reserved front row seating.

The highlight of the trip came when Oprah stopped to hug Squire, kissed his hand, and bubbled, "You're so cute!" says Tammy.

And what was Squire's take on his big day? "My three wishes came true," he says. "I always wanted fly in a plane, to ride in a limo, and to meet Oprah. It's the best time I have had in my life."

A resident at Golden Crest Nursing Home in Hibbing, MN, had given her son up for adoption when he was born. In her later years, she had corresponded with him but never seen him. When she was diagnosed with terminal cancer, her last wish was to finally meet her long-lost son.

One Saturday, her condition quickly worsened, and the associates at the home worked to contact her son. When they finally reached him, he said he was in between jobs, and just didn't have the money to travel to Hibbing. The sick resident was a single woman, who also didn't have many financial resources.

The associates knew how important this was to both mother and son, and got together to take up an emergency collection. One associate even drove 30 miles to Grand Rapids, MN, to wire the son money. The Golden Crest crew also talked to a motel owner in town, who they convinced to donate a room for the son for his stay.

The resident's daughter, who lives in the Twin Cities, also was notified of her mother's failing condition. Devastated and a bit frantic, she was able to arrange for someone to drive her the four hours to Hibbing, but she also was very short on money. Once again Golden Crest came to the rescue, wiring her expense money for the trip. The center also provided both son and daughter meals during their stay with their mother.

"Both were there at her bedside when she died on Sunday," says Barb Quitberg, director of nursing. "The associates efforts all came together and fell into place. It was all very touching."

The headline on Christmas morning would be a stunner: "Santa's Christmas Eve Run Postponed...Jolly Man Tied Up With Jury Duty."

Needless to say, the judge overseeing that case would be hard-pressed to find safe haven anywhere on the planet.

When Dave Detlefsen, who volunteers as Santa Claus at Neligh Nursing Center in Neligh, NE, was summoned to jury duty one cold December day, he decided to write a letter to the district judge pleading his case to be excused.

You see, he had a bit of a conflict later that month.

Wrote Dave, "I have been Santa in Neligh for about 25 years. I have always wanted to be able to serve jury duty, but am asking to be excused this time. Of course, I'll leave it up to you."

Says Donna Petersen, a recreation services director at the Neligh center, about Dave, "Christmas just wouldn't be the same at the Center without this jolly holiday man." The district judge, feeling the pressure—not to mention the weight of Neligh's children on his shoulders—finally relented. He stayed Santa's jury service, writing, "I am postponing your jury duty by reason of your duties as Santa for the children and elderly of Neligh. This is in the interest of community service. I also would not relish being known at the Grinch that kept Santa from Neligh."

The staff and residents of the Center wrote an article to thank the judge, which ran in a local newspaper. An excerpt, "Dave brings smiles, laughter and tears of joy to all of us each year, and our Christmas season would have been empty without him. You'll never know how much we appreciate your act of kindness."

Contributed by Beth Adair

Helping a Frustrated Customer Save Face

It can be easy for fast-food servers, under the gun, to quickly serve an endless sea of impatient customers, to shortchange or shunt aside those with special problems or needs—customers who risk slowing their assembly-line efficiency. But employees with the presence of mind and openness of heart to lend a hand in such special circumstances are those we tend to remember, and cherish.

I will never forget one such server I encountered at a Wendy's restaurant on University Avenue in St. Paul, MN. I was on my way to an evening meeting and running a bit ahead of schedule. So I thought I'd have enough time to stop in at a Wendy's for dinner. The line in the store looked short, so I pulled in.

Directly in front of me in line, a disheveled-looking woman with two young children waited at a register. The woman kept pointing to the items on the 99 cent menu, asking questions about each one. I could see the register employee getting frustrated with her questions. That's when the manager came out from the kitchen.

The manager first waved the next customer to the register, and then, smiling and friendly, proceeded to stand next to the menu and point to and explain each menu item to the woman and her children.

I was puzzled until I finally realized what he so clearly understood. With respect and dignity, this Wendy's manager gave his customer all the information she needed, without forcing her to admit that she couldn't read the menu.

Kristin Anderson

Going to Bat for the Bereaved

Customers are rarely more vulnerable than in the agony that follows the death of a loved one. Performing everyday duties and making decisions in the midst of this grief—such as securing travel arrangements—can take on momentous, even tortuous proportions. It takes special employees to both recognize this grief, and acknowledge it in a way that doesn't appear as "part of policy." Sometimes bereaved customers just want to be served quickly and efficiently, with a minimum of fuss. Other times, though, they welcome a shoulder to cry on.

The service pro easily distinguishes between the two.

The following two letters illustrate how vigilant employees from National Car Rental and Delta Airlines showed the kind of compassion and caring all employers might hope for in their people.

> TO: Terry Hardy
>
> National Car Rental
>
> Dear Mr. Hardy:
>
> I have flown over a million miles the last 15 years and have rented many automobiles during that time period. During that span there have been many "good and bad days." However, nothing comes close to the wonderful way I was treated by Joe Stabile at the National counter at the Grand Rapids Airport on Tuesday, May 30.
>
> Upon my arrival at the airport, I received a phone call advising me of a death in my family. When I arrived at the National counter, Joe observed something was wrong and asked if he could be of help. I explained what had just happened. He suggested I use the National office to collect my thoughts and to make any necessary phone calls. I told him it would be necessary for me to cancel my original car rental

plans and return immediately to Chicago. While I made a few local phone calls to cancel appointments, Joe checked with the local airlines to see if there was a Chicago flight available. I had just missed one. I then made the decision to drive to Chicago. Joe had someone drive a rental car to the curb, while I made some additional phone calls and also had them place my luggage in the trunk.

When I was ready to leave, he told me the cost of the car rental to Chicago would be picked up by National. I said that wouldn't be necessary and it wouldn't be fair, since I planned to keep the car for 3 or 4 days until the funeral was concluded. Joe then worked out a special rate of $18 a day for the use of the Oldsmobile Cutlass from Tuesday through Sunday morning.

The treatment I received from Joe Stabile was more than a client taking care of a customer. It was obvious this is his "way of life." National Car Rental should consider itself fortunate to have such a person in its employ.

I have told this story to forty or fifty people in the past week. There have been many wonderful comments—from "You don't hear of that happening these days," to my son-in-law, who said it best when he commented, "Wouldn't it be great if everyone in the world responded each day to their respective daily problems the same way this gentlemen did? Wouldn't our world be a much better place to live?"

Kindest regards,

Thomas J. Brueck
Bill Communications

To: Ron Allen

President, Delta Airlines

Atlanta, GA

Dear Mr. Allen:

I am writing this letter to express my deepest appreciation for the service I was given by Delta Airlines and especially, Gail DiCicco, a flight attendant. I was on a business trip in Vancouver on December 10, 1996 when my husband called me at 5:15 A.M. with the devastating news that my thirty-six-year-old brother had collapsed and died playing basketball, leaving a widow and two small children. I was scheduled to leave Vancouver the next day, but wanted to get home immediately on the 7 A.M. flight. My colleague and I quickly packed and reached the airport at 6 A.M. As I was waiting, a ticket agent from your commuter airline approached us and said, "You look like you need help. What can I do?" He scheduled us on our desired flight in a quick and efficient manner.

I then proceeded to customs and behind me was Gail DiCicco, a flight attendant on the same flight. As we waited to go through customs, I explained what had happened and how grateful I was to get on the flight and home to my family. She put her arms around me and told me how sorry she was. Once I got on the plane, the flight attendant at the door asked if I had been talking with a flight attendant (Gail) earlier. When I said yes, she told my colleague and I we could sit in first class where Gail was working. Throughout the whole flight, Gail was attentive, compassionate, and a good listener. To me, she embodies what service is all about. I hope your company has some form of recognition that rewards people like Gail. She is someone who can do her job, and do it with soul! This also reaffirms my belief that Delta is the only airline to fly.

Sincerely,

Sue Showers
Hamilton County Educational Service Center

The Great Floods of '97

As we go to press, the Red River of the North has receded into the confines of its age-old banks. But the devastation wrought by its 60-day rampage-cresting 26 feet above flood stage on April 21, 1997—is far from ended. Farms and fields, streets and homes disappeared as the river's unrelenting sweep destroyed dikes, dams, and lives. The cities of Grand Forks, ND, and East Grand Forks, MN, were ravaged not only by the raging floodwater, but by fire as well. Four square blocks in the heart of Grand Forks burned as firefighters could only watch.

Tens of thousands were forced out of their homes. In many cases evacuees literally raced from their homes, steps in front of the surging waters. Thousands of people fled with only the clothes on their backs and the change in their pockets. Automobiles, valuables, favorite mementos were abandoned, and either washed away by the advancing waters or turned to rubbish. The capital toll to date exceeds $1 billion. The human toll exceeds calculation.

Many have rushed into the breech with aid and support. The American Red Cross and Salvation Army have been on hand with day-to-day sustenance and support since the emergency began. FEMA (the Federal Emergency Management Agency) has set up shop and is sorting out federal aid qualifiers.

But beyond the headlines and out of the range of nightly news cameras, thousands of acts of extraordinary compassion and quiet heroism took place. Organizations and individuals were moved to bring aid and comfort to those whose lives were so disrupted. A compendium of these acts—big and small—would fill a library.

- Though dozens of radio and television news outlets provided live coverage of the flood, the *Grand Forks Herald*, the local paper, kept publishing despite flooding and severe fire damage to its main offices. Employees simply relocated to another building on dry ground and set up a makeshift newsroom. The paper's short-term goals: To provide information on the fate of friends and acquaintances, and give a sense of hope and stability to residents.

- U.S. West employees barricaded themselves behind a wall of sandbags inside their central switching office in downtown Grand Forks in order to maintain service. Phone calls to out-of-service numbers were all forwarded to wherever subscribers had been able to find temporary shelter. The National Guard boated in food and water during the siege.

- AirTouch Communications and Cellular One, the area's cellular service providers, donated phones and service to police, firefighters, National Guardsmen, and other emergency workers. Over 700 phones in all—plus air time—were donated.

- On-air personalities from twenty-one Minneapolis-St. Paul radio stations gathered at the downtown Minneapolis Target Center and entreated listeners to drive by and make donations of dollars and goods. By the end of the day, listeners had dropped off 35 semi-tractor/trailer loads of goods—and half a million dollars in cash. Thirty-one Rainbow Foods stores—a local grocery chain—served as repositories for donations of goods, as did the 431 stores at the Mall of America and 10 area Target stores. The resulting truck caravan stretched for miles.

- In the Minnesota city of Red Wing, the Red Wing Shoe Company filled its trucks to the brim with company products—shoes, boots, pants, hats, and coats—and other locally donated goods and joined the convoy.

- Pillsbury Co., General Mills, Cargill, Malt-O-Meal, and Fabio Foods donated truckloads of food to Second Harvest food banks for distribution. Hershey's, Heinz, Procter & Gamble, Kraft, and M&M Mars also sent food banks truckloads of product earmarked for Grand Forks distribution.

- Supervalu, Midwest Coca Cola Bottling, and Culligan Co. trucked bottled water to the area until the local water systems were operating again.

- Northwest Airlines made a 747 available to volunteers from area companies; the volunteers helped load and airlift 220,000 pounds of donated goods to the scene. Another aircraft was made available to airlift clean-up volunteers to the area. Later, the airline made unrestricted $49 fares available to fatigued Grand Forks residents who wanted to escape the area for a few days of R&R.

- Companies such as Dayton-Hudson, St. Paul Cos., and 3M gave employees time off to join volunteer groups to assist in the aftermath clean up.

- Banks throughout the region established relief funds and continuously advertised their availability, urging customers to make contributions—and many of the banks pledged to match customer largess.

The outpourings of assistance were not restricted to corporations and relief agencies, nor were they only local and regional in scope.

- Ukrops Grocery stores in Richmond, VA, asked customers to make food donations, which the company matched and shipped to Grand Forks in their own over-the-road trucks.

- An individual, anonymous benefactor in California—referred to simply as "Angel" (later identified as Joan Kroc, wife of McDonald's founder Ray Kroc) sent $10 million to be distributed in chunks of $2,000 to families in need of out-of-pocket expenses. When need outstripped funds, an unnamed corporation added $5 million more to the stipend.

- The town of Bemidji, MN, offered shelter to 2,000 evacuees and 1,300 families in the Bemidji area, they simply handed over the keys to their summer cabins and lake cottages to relief coordinators. In many of the town's gas stations, pharmacies, and restaurants, the evacuees were simply given whatever they needed; tanks and prescriptions filled, restaurant tabs comped, and so on. A local bank handed out emergency funds to any who requested them.

- Evacuees Tim and Lori Pesch were grocery shopping in a Bemidji grocery store when another shopper recognized Tim's East Grand Forks High School t-shirt. She walked up to them, pressed a crumpled $100 bill in Tim's hand, and wished them well.

- Dee and Troy Christensen were so moved by the tragedy of the Grand Forks flood that they offered room in their home to displaced families. The Christensens live in Phoenix, AZ—1,875 miles from Grand Forks. "From the images on the TV, it looks like a disaster zone," Dee Christensen said. "I just cannot imagine it, having your house full of water. My heart just went out to those people." The couple has no connections to North Dakota or Minnesota. They were just amazed by the spirit and tenacity of the people who they read about and watched on television coverage of the disaster.

- At least 200 precious family pets were left behind as the water rose and people rushed to evacuate their homes when the dikes let go Friday, April 18. By Saturday afternoon, Terri Crist and a team from the Emergency Animal Rescue Service were on the ground in Grand Forks, ready to begin retrieving pets from homes caught in the water. By the time the waters had receded they had rescued more than 200 animals.

If bad times and natural disasters bring out the best in people, then there was a second, intangible, but wholly palpable flood in Grand Forks; a flood of service from the heart who's high crest is yet to be marked.

Compiled from various news sources

Jessie's Glove

Rick Phillips does a lot of management training each year for the Circle K Corp., a national chain of convenience stores. Among the topics he addresses in seminars is the retention of quality employees—a real challenge to managers when you consider the pay scale in the service industry. During these discussions, he asks participants, "What has caused you to stay long enough to become a manager?"

Some time back a new manager took the question and slowly, with her voice almost breaking, said, "It was a $19 baseball glove."

We'll let Rick tell the rest of the story as he did in *Chicken Soup for the Soul at Work* :

"Cynthia originally took a job at Circle K as an interim position while she looked for something better. On her second or third day behind the counter, she received a phone call from her nine-year-old son, Jessie. He needed a baseball glove for Little League. Cynthia explained that as a single mother, money was very tight, and her first check would have to go for paying bills. Perhaps she could buy his baseball glove with her second or third check.

"When Cynthia arrived for work that next morning, Patricia, the store manager, asked her to come to the small room in the back of the store that served as an office. Cynthia wondered if she had done something wrong or left some part of her job incomplete from the day before. She was concerned and confused.

Patricia handed her a box. "I overheard you talking to your son yesterday," she said, "And I know that it's hard to explain things to kids. This is a baseball glove for Jessie because he may not understand how important he is even though you have to pay bills before you have to buy gloves. You know we can't pay good people like you as much as we would like to, but we do care, and I want you to know how important you are to us."

The thoughtfulness, empathy, and love of this convenience store manager demonstrates how vividly many people remember more how much an employer cares, than how much an employer pays.

An important lesson for the price of a Little League baseball glove.

Contributed by Rick Phillips

Officers of the Law Need Kind Words, Too

While awaiting his son's arrival at Charlotte Douglas International Airport, Larry Rouse of Charlotte, NC, sat in his car at a "No Parking" passenger loading zone. When his son didn't appear, Larry went inside to check the flight schedule, only to return to find a ticket on his windshield. Shoving the ticket into his pocket, he realized that he'd left his car keys in the terminal and went back to get them.

When he came back, he found a second ticket on his windshield.

A police officer stood several feet away. "Officer," he pleaded, "I really do deserve the first ticket, but would you please take back the second?" When Larry explained the situation, the officer said "Sure" and plucked the ticket back from his hand. At this point, Larry's son arrived. "We were about to drive away when the officer walked up," he says. "Afraid that he'd had a change of heart, I rolled down the window with some trepidation."

"You know," the officer began, "I appreciate the way you spoke to me. Most people aren't quite so kind. Let me tear up the first ticket, too. And have a good day."

Reader's Digest

An Angel's Kiss?

You've just had a major heart attack, lost consciousness, and needed resuscitation to keep you breathing. You awake in a hazy, dream-like state, not quite sure if you're in this world or the next. Suddenly you feel a warm pressure on your forehead...

Oregon Health Sciences University was in a major crunch for beds in the summer of 1996. It was so bad, in fact, that the hospital finally had to admit some adult patients to one of its pediatric units. One of those adult patients had just had a cardiac arrest and required resuscitation. A pediatric nurse stayed with the patient during the difficult procedure and recovery. When his vital signs were restored but he was still unconscious, she leaned down and softly kissed his forehead, telling him all was well and that he was going to be okay. On some level, she thought, "he can hear me".

Back at home a few weeks later, the patient wrote to Patricia Southard at OHSU. "He remembers that soft kiss, and that gentle voice telling him he was going to be fine. It was only at that point he knew he'd made it, and that indeed he was going to be okay," says Patricia.

Contributed by Patricia Southard

Star the Wonder Dog

In 1989 we wrote a book entitled *The Service Edge: 101 Companies that Profit from Customer Care* . We asked readers, as we always do, to tell us what they thought of the book and our list of super service companies. We had our hands full fielding the response from people who wanted to tell us about their own favorite companies and most memorable service experiences.

The letter I remember most vividly arrived in a white, #9 envelope—with colorful dog-themed ink stamps all over it. Dog bones, dog paws, dog heads—not your typical business letter. I double checked to make sure this envelope was really addressed to our office. It was. Curiosity peaked, I quickly opened it to see who it was from.

The signature read: Kathy Diamond Davis, Pet Therapist.

As I read her letter, I discovered that Kathy's work didn't involve counseling Spot on how to get along better with Puff, but rather she used her specially trained dogs to work with autistic children and Alzheimer's patients.

Kathy had purchased a copy of *The Service Edge* because she sees herself as a professional service provider. "After all," she wrote, "I serve a dog who serves people. I have to love what I do!"

Kathy was writing to add a plaudit to one of the airlines we'd written about in the book—American Airlines.

Kathy explained that the dog she works for, most frequently, was actually born and raised in Denver—not in Oklahoma City, where she does her good works. When this dog was about nine months old, the family raising her had a new baby, and due to some medical complications could no longer keep the dog in their home. The family wanted to place the dog where she could do the therapy work she was trained for, and which fit her personality so well. They put the word out to the pet therapy community, and Kathy jumped at the chance to take the dog into her home, her practice, and her heart.

But it was December and Kathy didn't feel she could drive all the way to Denver from Oklahoma City in uncertain road conditions to collect the dog. So she arranged to have the dog shipped by air.

When Kathy and her husband went to the airport to pick the dog up, they waited—and waited, and waited, and waited. But no dog carrier emerged from the double doors in the baggage claim. Kathy finally flagged a baggage claim clerk. "He wasn't very interested in helping—until I explained that I'd insured the dog for $500," Kathy wrote. He went back to search for the dog.

Eventually, the clerk discovered that the dog mistakenly had been placed on a flight to Chicago's O'Hare Airport. To get the dog flown back to Oklahoma City, the poor canine would have to be transported and jostled all the way around the airport, out onto the cold tarmac, and Kathy wasn't sure how she'd survive the trip.

She didn't give the clerk time to explain further. She started calling other airlines at O'Hare to see if they could help her out. All said no, using some rationale along the lines of "I'm sorry, but since you didn't book with us in the first place, there's really nothing we can do now." Until, that is, she reached Brenda at American Airlines. "It was as if Brenda threw me a life line," Kathy wrote. "I didn't have to explain that losing my dog was a bit different from losing a piece of luggage." She empathized with Kathy's concern. "Give me 20 minutes and I'll call you back and let you know what we can do," Brenda said.

Some 15 minutes later, Brenda called. She'd located the dog and was having it transferred into American Airlines' custody. She'd identified a flight to Oklahoma City and promised the dog would be on it. And, she asked Kathy to call her when the dog arrived, "Just so I'll know she got in all right."

Sure enough, Kathy traveled back to the airport, and was greeted by the wonderful sight of a dog carrier bursting through the baggage claim doors.

Kathy forgot to call Brenda, but later that day—you guessed it—Brenda called her. "Hi, I checked with the agent in Oklahoma City, so I know the dog got off the flight okay. But I still wanted to hear from you that she was all right."

And in case you're wondering what Kathy named her new partner? "I named her Star, because she was my Christmas miracle from American Airlines," she says.

Kristin Anderson

Passing the Hat for a Troubled Customer

On January 21, 1997, Warren Foreman and Troy Sanchez, two meter readers for the Denver Water Co., were doing some readings on their regular route when an elderly lady poked her head out of a nearby home. She asked for help, explaining that she hadn't had any running water for over a week. That wasn't all, she said, she had also been without heat since mid-December—more than a full month in freezing conditions. Warren and Troy went into her house to investigate—and found over four feet of water in a crawl space. Her pipes had frozen and burst, in subzero temperatures the previous week. They also noticed she was using her oven for heat, and she had little food in her kitchen. As they became more aware of the setting, they realized the inside of her home was generally pretty run down.

They called their dispatcher, who contacted the Fire Department to begin the task of pumping water out of the crawl space. After learning of the generally desperate situation Warren and Troy had discovered, their supervisor placed a call to the Social Services Department to lend a hand to the situation as well.

When Warren and Troy returned to the office, they had a hard time forgetting about the elderly customer's plight. They asked their supervisor if they could take up a collection from their co-workers to buy the woman groceries and bottled water. They collected over $150 from field personnel, and workers in the customer services office chipped in another $100. Part of the donated funds were applied to her water bill. When the groceries and other goods were delivered, the astonished customer broke out into a wide smile.

But the people at Denver Water wanted to do even more. Another field worker, Jon Martinez, a licensed and bonded plumber, repaired the customer's service line, at no charge.

Materials for the job were donated by the utility's plumbing shop, including some leftover copper pipe and connectors from other plumbing jobs. Lyle Eckart, another field rep, gave Jon a hand with the repairs. These were no balmy conditions the two toiled in either—it was a cold, muddy crawl space overrun with spiders.

Pending further repairs and clean up of the property, the customer was temporarily moved from the home by the Denver Social Services Department. But not before she, and another relative the department had contacted to lend her a hand, took time to visit and thank the Denver Water crew for its concern and above-the-call support during a very difficult time.

Contributed by Cheri M. Garton

Remembering the Rescue Dogs of Oklahoma City

Following the 1995 bombing of the Alfred P. Murrah federal building in Oklahoma City, the entire country seemed immersed in stories about the disaster. Employees of Hill's Pet Nutrition, Inc., in Topeka, KS, were no exception. Their hearts reached out, but like many others, they weren't sure what they could do to help. When a group of Hill's employees gathered to brainstorm about options, they naturally thought about ways to aid and comfort the relatives of blast victims. But as makers of pet foods, they also thought about helping the silent, unsung heroes of the tragedy: the specially-trained dogs assisting with recovery efforts at the site.

Before long, a group of technicians at the Topeka plant had arranged for 40,000 pounds of pet food to be donated and transported to the bomb site to feed the rescue dogs. "It was a great idea and the least we could do," says Bob Wheeler, Hill's CEO.

But that wasn't all. Hill's employees also took up a collection of money to be given to families in need. The company then matched the employees' contributions. A check for nearly $4,000 was presented in Oklahoma City, along with the load of pet food, within a week following the tragedy.

Contributed by Kathy Davis

Wal-Mart Cares About Kids

Most often, service from the heart is a person-to-person display of compassion and caring. One or two or a half-dozen people extending themselves to help others through a time of extreme need or trauma. It is humanity in its purist form.

So it is difficult to visualize or imagine service from the heart coming in a corporate wrapper. But there is no other way to characterize Wal-Mart's nationwide Code Adam program than as a corporate-wide act of service from the heart.

Code Adam is named in remembrance of six-year-old Adam Walsh, whose 1981 abduction from a Florida shopping mall and subsequent murder brought the tragedy of child abduction into the national consciousness. Code Adam is a special alert issued over the public address system when a customer reports a missing child in a Wal-Mart store or a SAM's Club. A brief description of the child is provided to all associates, who immediately stop their normal work to look for the child. Store associates also monitor all exits to ensure the lost child does not leave the store.

If the child is not found within 10 minutes, or if the child is seen accompanied by someone other than a parent or guardian, the local police department is contacted for assistance.

The Code Adam program began when Bill Burns, a Wal-Mart employee, read a newspaper article about an attempted abduction in a shopping mall in Indianapolis, IN. His idea, a special in-store public address code to be used in the event of an abduction or attempted abduction, was given its name by another employee, Dawn Love, of the Wal-Mart store in Crawfordsville, IN. Love and a team from her store worked out the criteria and action steps for a Code Adam alert. The process they designed is now in place in all Wal-Mart stores and SAM's Clubs.

How has Code Adam worked?

- In November 1993, the procedure stopped the attempted abduction of a three-year-old girl from a Wal-Mart store in Crawfordsville, where the procedure was invented. The abductor, who had a prior record of child abduction, was arrested and later convicted.

- In September 1995, a seven-year-old girl disappeared while shopping with her parents at a Wal-Mart in Pascagoalo, MI. The store's Code Adam policy kicked in, and the search began. By 6 o'clock the following morning, the child was recovered safely, a state away. Police credit the Wal-Mart program with alerting them to the crime in time to prevent a tragedy.

Good people acting in concert *can* make important things happen and even save lives—even in the largest organizations. For more information about the Code Adam program, visit Wal-Mart's community involvement website at: www.Wal-Mart.com. The complete procedure, along with a history of the program is located there.

Excerpted from http://www.Wal-Mart.com

5

At Risk of Life and Limb

There are people who, by the nature of their work, routinely put themselves between others and disaster. Police and security guards, firefighters, and paramedics come quickly to mind, as do National Guard, American Red Cross, and Salvation Army workers, who, in times of natural disaster, come riding to the rescue.

We marvel at their deeds and wonder at their nerve. We are as grateful to them as we are mystified by their grit and steadiness.

The *Cops* and *911 Emergency* television programs that show these everyday heroes in action remind us how special they are and how admirable—and often dangerous to carry out—are their everyday deeds.

From time to time, chance, accident, being in the right—or wrong—place at the right time, can bring those of us with more mundane expectations of our work—and ourselves—face-to-face with equally challenging opportunities and make us participants, at least temporarily, in life on the dramatic side.

The tales in this chapter highlight customer service people who have been called up by circumstance to reach out beyond the narrow confines of their jobs and help another human being who, at least for that moment in time, could not help him or herself. Some of their deeds are truly lifesaving and heroic. Others are acts of gentler rescue, but are nonetheless acts of personal extension well above and beyond any reasonable work-a-day world expectations. We marvel at these individuals just as we marvel at those who have consciously given themselves over to a calling clearly defined by the simple motto, "To Serve and Protect." And we hope that we see within their unusual and unexpected acts of valor or personal extension and compassion, some shadow, some premonition of ourselves; some resonant hint of how we might also respond if similarly challenged.

Insurance Reps Create Unique Road Rescue

When Cheryl Glenn, a Blue Cross and Blue Shield of Minnesota telephone service rep, showed up for work that Friday in August, she never expected to be saving someone's life. Answering questions, steering customers through the maze of their health care coverage, maybe even calming an upset or unhappy customer, sure, but never saving someone's life.

Shortly before 9 A.M., Cheryl received a call from a man who said he needed to know which doctor he could see with his Blue Cross/Blue Shield coverage. As Cheryl was verifying the man's policy number, she became aware that he was having difficulty reading the numbers aloud to her. The reason became obvious when he gasped: "Can I go to Unity Hospital? I think I'm having a heart attack."

Though taken aback, Cheryl stayed calm and focused on the man's condition. "Please don't go anywhere," she told him, "Stay where you are, I'll call 911." To her dismay, the advice was a little late, "I'm not at home. I'm in my car," he answered, then reassured Cheryl that he had pulled off the road to call.

Cheryl then flagged co-worker Julie Johnson to place the call to 911, while she kept the man on the line. As Julie called in the man's location and situation, Cheryl kept the man engaged—and busy. "I remembered when I was pregnant with my son, I had high blood pressure and was told to lie on my left side to take stress off my heart. So I told him if he could, he should try to lean to his left side."

By this time, the man was becoming incoherent and began insisting that he should drive himself to the hospital. Cheryl patiently and repeatedly explained that he must wait for help to arrive and that his best course of action was preserving his strength.

Things took a nasty turn when Cheryl suddenly realized the man had incorrectly identified his location; he was not on Highway 36 but on Interstate 35-E. Johnson quickly amended the directions she'd supplied to the highway patrol.

When Cheryl asked the man who she might notify for him, he said he wanted Cheryl to contact his sister, but he couldn't remember her last name or phone number. He did, however, remember his co-worker Brian's phone number, and Julie immediately contacted him. "Their conversation lasted about two seconds. Brian said he was on his way and hung up," Cheryl recalls.

Brian reached the gentleman even before the highway patrol. Cheryl, who was still on the line comforting the man, spoke to Brian and they agreed that she should hang up so the highway patrol could get a from-the-scene description of the man's condition.

As she set the phone receiver back in its place, her mask of composure washed away, and her eyes welled up with tears. With limbs of Jell-O and thoughts filled with unanswered questions, Cheryl felt numb. She recalls, "I didn't feel like I made a difference because I still didn't know if he was going to be okay."

This incredible story does not end there. Throughout the day, Cheryl received updates from the man's employer. She was informed that the man was near death when he arrived at the hospital, but an emergency room medical team had managed to revive him. Later in the day Cheryl learned that he was okay and resting comfortably in the intensive care unit.

Now that she's had a chance to rethink the ordeal, Cheryl believes she did "okay" under pressure. "Even though we never spoke again, I have a very good, self-satisfying feeling about the whole thing—I'm just glad I could help."

Contributed by Teresa Novacek

No Ordinary Public Utility Guys, These!

Chasing down fugitives or keeping a gasping heart pumping aren't exactly skill sets found in your average meter reader's job description. But that didn't stop Art Castro or Jody Godsey from putting their own safety on the line to help two customers in dire need.

While conducting an audit at a customer's residence in October 1996, Art, a water conservation specialist for the City of Tucson, Arizona, Water Department, noticed a number of police cars gathered in the neighborhood. Not much later, a woman hanging out laundry at her nearby home called out to him, saying there was a suspicious-looking man in her backyard. Sure enough, when Art came over and looked through her bathroom window, he saw a man crawling on his hands and knees toward the house.

It turns out police weren't gathered for an informal confab; they were conducting a dragnet in the surrounding area, trying to snare a wanted criminal—the man in the backyard.

The customer held her baby, terrified. Rather than calling out to the police, Art advised her to keep her family in the house and lock all the doors.

Then, Art ran back into the yard to confront the fugitive.

"I ran around the opposite side of the house, and he came running right at me," Art says. "I blocked him off from a gate, jumped at him and kind of body tackled him, holding him down." By this time, the police were on the scene. But the fugitive wasn't through yet, even after Art's harsh lesson in the physics of motion.

"We had him down, but he got up for a moment and tried to dart off again," Art says. "When I watched the cops pull out their guns to stop him, that's when reality set in. I had to ask myself what the heck I was doing there."

Says Art now about his actions, "I was just doing my job. Had there not been any danger to the woman and her children, I probably would have stayed inside with the homeowner's family."

Contributed by Mitch Basefsky

Jody Godsey's 1997 had an unusual start. On January 2, during his rounds as a meter reader for United Water Florida of Jacksonville, he heard a commotion and some voices at the front of a nearby home. He looked around the corner to see two men arguing fiercely on the front lawn. Then, one man collapsed to the ground as the other fled on foot.

Jody ran over to lend assistance, and saw that the collapsed man wasn't breathing, and had a blue look. He flagged down a passer-by, asked him to call 911, and quickly began administering CPR. The paramedics arrived within 10 minutes and took over, spiriting the man off to the emergency room. Jody, his adrenaline still pumping, was left wondering if the customer had survived the ordeal. "I still had a couple hundred meters to read, but I kept thinking about him," he says. "His coloring looked so bad I didn't think he'd make it."

A week later, Jody got his answer. The customer's daughter had heard about the "heroic meter reader" and called Jody to say her father had survived the confrontation, and she wanted to thank him for saving his life. She said he was scheduled to return home from the hospital that week, and also said the paramedics told her had Jody not been on the spot and known what to do, her father probably wouldn't have made it. She went on to say that, although her father was having difficulty speaking, some of his first words when he regained consciousness were "meter reader."

"A huge weight was lifted when I got that call," he says.

Jody, a new employee, had received CPR and first aid certification through the company just 4 months before the incident.

Contributed by Lisa Parks

Into Harm's Way: Two Tales of Hurricane Heroics

Screaming 100-mile-per-hour winds, battering rains, flying debris—and your world turned upside down. The middle of a world-class hurricane, and under the real threat of bodily extinction, is among the last places you'd expect people to keep their service heads screwed on straight and stay vigilant to customers' needs.

But where the service ethic becomes ingrained, it shows its face regardless of the situation, sometimes on auto pilot. In the three cases profiled, good service—and no small dose of courage—filtered through a hurricane's raging winds and rain, the lack of food and water, bad tempers and even threat of death. Somehow, employees were able to subdue their fears and make the abnormal seem normal to their frightened customers.

Jack Thomas, an administrator for Hercules Aerospace Co., spent 36 hours with his wife in the exposed hallway of a Cancun, Mexico hotel while Hurricane Gilbert terrorized the area in 1988.

We'll let Jack recall in his own words how the hotel staff shone brightly throughout those tense hours.

"Our hosts were the most gracious, concerned, and caring people. The power failed and somehow they found candles. The water stopped and bottled water suddenly appeared. Our room was filled with sand and water...and the hotel staff provided us with everything we needed to clean up. That evening the hotel somehow managed to get a gas stove working and fixed all the guests Mexican spaghetti. The next morning...scrambled eggs and ham, again at no charge. After breakfast, one of the employees took some of us into town in his car to one of the few working supermarkets."

The cessation of the howling winds didn't mean the end of the top-notch treatment, however, Jack says. "Our charter flight home was delayed one day due to hurricane damage at the airport. Representatives of Mexican Morris, the airline, treated us like family. A sack lunch was waiting on every seat as we boarded, and once boarded we were told that all drinks were on Morris. We were all given free `I survived Gilbert' t-shirts and a free ticket to a choice of destinations.

"I will go back to Cancun, and I will fly Morris airlines. If they are willing to stick their necks out for their customers under those conditions, then I will be comfortable in the knowledge that I can expect only first-class treatment in normal situations."

Hurricane Fran roared ashore on the Carolina coast, causing massive damage up and down that state. Mitchell's Formal Wear stores at the Crabtree Valley and Cary Village Square Malls in Raleigh, NC, somehow managed to keep their doors open—and customers happy. Store managers Franc Sabino and Claudia Goodson, working together, were able to weather the storm and deliver unusually high-quality service.

The day after the hurricane, Mitchell's was among but a handful of stores still open. Even the local post office—and you're familiar with their motto—had closed down. "We had no electricity, and my store resembled a church, with all the candles we had lit," remembers Sabino, manager of the Cary location. "Still, we were able to give our customers the service they've come to expect—and in a much more romantic setting!"

The store at the Crabtree Valley Mall was under nearly four feet of water when Claudia attempted to get in—no easy task, because Mitchell's doesn't supply its managers with rubber rafts. So Franc, in contact with Claudia, tried to recreate all the customer orders for her store and have them sent to his store. One small problem: contacting the customers about the change. Phone service was out in most areas, and customer phone numbers were in the Crabtree store, which by this time was behind police lines.

So, the next day, Claudia jumped the police barricade and got into her store, which had no lights. In complete darkness, she grabbed most of the tuxedos off the rack and started the journey to her car. On the way there, she commandeered a Ford Bronco from a bystander who knew better than to refuse her request—the driver was getting married that same day, and his tuxedo was on Claudia's rolling rack.

Says Franc, "Claudia arrived at my store with her rack of tuxedos and customer names, and by then I did have lights again. We handled customers from both locations at the little Cary store, as well as a few of our competitor's customers. At the very end of an exhausting day, we were proud to say that all of our customers were satisfied—and our cash drawer balanced."

Contributed by Matt Childs

UPS Highway Heroes Save Lives

It's not unusual for the omnipresent brown-clad messengers, drivers of the 147,000 vehicles of the United Parcel Service, to see accidents or emergency situations as they log over 2 billion miles a year delivering some 3 billion packages and witness a lot of `life-on-the-road.' What is a bit remarkable is their willingness to pull over and lend a hand to others in need, even amidst their own daunting delivery deadlines.

Enough UPS drivers regularly go out of their way to aid strangers, in fact, that they often find themselves in line for awards.

In 1996, five UPS employees were honored for lifesaving actions by Liberty Mutual Insurance Company's Life Saver's Award. And two, Jeffrey May and Clinton LeFabvre, were also finalists in Goodyear Tire Co.'s 1996 National Highway Hero Program. Liberty Mutual established its Life Saver's Award Program in 1922 to honor people responsible for saving a human life; UPS has been insured by Liberty Mutual Insurance since 1932.

Launched in 1983, the Goodyear award program is an effort to elevate the image and public awareness of the responsible elements in the transportation industry.

Here are some of the UPS employees so honored, and their heroic acts.

- On May 22, 1996, Jerry Florkowski of South Bend, IN, pulled three people from a burning car and then continued on his package delivery route. Onlookers could identify the hero only as a "UPS driver." Florkowski later came forward, saying he was thinking of his own daughter and unborn grandchild's fatal accident that occurred only 7 weeks earlier when he put his life on the line.

- On February 23, 1996, Jeffrey May of Guilford, CT, and Clint LeFabvre of Laconia, NH, were driving along Interstate I-495 in Chelmsford, MA, when they came upon a fiery crash. The two UPS men worked together to rescue one of the drivers—less than 20 seconds before the car exploded into flames. Then May and LeFabvre searched in dense fog for the other vehicle involved in the accident. They found the cab of the tractor-trailer truck in a tree off the highway, then climbed the tree to free the injured driver.

- Mark J. Sladick of Springboro, PA, was making a delivery at a residence on March 21, 1996. When he approached the front door, he noticed a woman lying on the floor of her home. Sladick entered the house, called 911, and began administering CPR. The woman resumed breathing before the paramedics arrived.

- In February 1996, a woman and her baby arrived at the front counter of UPS's Chatham, Canada facility to pick up a package. Suddenly, the toddler began to show signs of distress and choking. UPS's Mike Doran ran to the child and administered the Heimlich maneuver. Thanks to Doran's quick action, the toddler was soon back to normal.

Says Tom Walsh, UPS corporate health and safety manager, "The willingness of these employees to go above and beyond the call of duty by helping individuals in need is a credit to UPS. We are very proud of all our heroes."

Contributed by Kristen Petrella

Little Things Sometimes Mean More Than a Lot

If you fly Southwest Airlines you know. You know about the low fares, the first-come-first-serve seating and the slightly wacky ways of some of the employees. And if you've read the book *NUTS!* by Kevin and Jackie Freiberg, you know that there is a genuine lust for great service that begins with Southwest Chairman Herb Kelleher and permeates the whole organization. Recently, leafing through a sheaf of letters from Southwest customers shared with us by Anne Bruce, manager of the airline's University for People, we came across one letter that sums up the organization and its relentless passion to serve customers.

Dear Mr. Kelleher and Ms. Barrett,

For many years my husband, John, and I have taken for granted the way that Southwest Airlines works. We took the big things for granted (like the "friends fly free" program, which meant I could travel with him on business on "The Company Plane" for less than he could fly on another airline alone), as well as the little things like the many laughs we would have relating stories of jokes told by flight attendants over the PA, the fun we had playing gate games during flight delays, the smiles from reindeer horns worn by the flight crews at Christmas time, the way flight attendants serving us, while making several hops, would remember exactly what we were drinking, the birthday cards, and the consistently friendly service from all your employees.

However, in October we had an experience that prompts us to let you know how much we appreciate Southwest's commitment to customer service. John was hopping across the Southwest on a week-long business trip. On October 10, 1996, while visiting Kingman, AZ, (via a Southwest flight from San Francisco to Las Vegas), he became very ill. We assumed that he had food poisoning. He called the company travel agent who said the only way home was on an American Airlines connection through Dallas with a 90-minute layover. He placed a call directly to Southwest reservations and they were able to find one seat open on WN524, a nonstop to Kansas City.

John headed for the Las Vegas airport, he got the last seat on the plane, made it on in the first boarding group, sat in the back closest to the lavatory, and waited for take-off. He became violently ill as the plane was taxiing. The flight attendants immediately offered assistance. During the flight home he was ill many times, even losing his glasses down the toilet. Through it all, with a plane bursting with passengers, the flight attendants did what they could, even sending him off the plane with a "sick bag" for the trip home in the car.

I took John to the hospital 30 minutes after landing. The initial diagnosis was not food poisoning, but diabetic ketoacidosis. The doctor told me that he might've been in a coma or dead within another hour. That timely flight may have saved his life. Two days later, after many tests, they found that he had suffered a "silent" massive heart attack, probably in Kingman. The illness was secondary to that incident. (The doctors did not suspect a heart attack because he is only 41 years old.) He had angioplasty and is recovering fully, working out for an hour every day, back at work full time.

We want to say a special thank you to Southwest for:

- the courtesy and kindness extended to John on that diffi-cult flight;
- having a reservation system so accurate that it could find one open seat;
- having timely, frequent nonstop flights available;
- for all the big and little things we have taken for granted over the years!

Happy Holidays to everyone at Southwest Airlines!

Kathleen Foster

Liberty, Missouri

The $800 Thank-You Letter

Paul Olson was so pleased with what doctors at the Mayo Clinic did to help save his life, he rented a billboard to thank them.

Olson's thank-you note is hard to miss in downtown Rochester, MN, home of the renowned clinic on the prairie. It's a dramatic $800 message on a 12 x 25 foot billboard: "Dear Mayo Clinic: Thanks for Five Years of Life...—A Surviving Cancer Patient."

Olson, president of the Blandin Foundation in Grand Rapids, MN, said the message carries "my effort at public education," as well as his gratitude to medical workers who sometimes think that their tasks are thankless.

Olson was 47 in 1992 when the clinic caught his prostrate cancer through a prostrate specific antigen blood test, which some insurers have resisted covering for men under 50 because it sometimes produces false-positive readings.

"I am eternally grateful to Mayo for practicing medicine their way, and not the way of the insurance companies," said Olson. "If you catch it early, young guys, old guys can be just fine...We've just got to get more guys into routine checking."

Mayo spokesman John La Forgia said the thank-you billboard is a first for Rochester as far as he knows, and has become a conversation piece at the clinic.

"It certainly makes people feel good that a patient was so pleased with his care here," he said.

Contributed by Robert Franklin
Excerpted from
Minneapolis Star Tribune (May 18, 1997)

No Deposit = No Service?
Not to This Southern Bell Rep

Carol Mavigliano is a service representative in the Southern Bell office in West Palm Beach, FL. In the course of a typical day, she handles dozens of calls from current and new customers. A few years back, one of those calls was from the daughter of a seventy-one-year-old man who was living alone and needed to have phone service established. Among other things, the daughter said he was a diabetic and had a serious heart condition—the telephone represented his lifeline to emergency medical assistance. But he also was living on a limited income and didn't have the money for the deposit required.

What should the daughter do?

As it turned out, she'd already done the right thing by hooking up with a representative to whom service was more than a job. Not only did Carol get the new hookup order processed without a deposit, she set it up so the phone would be installed the next day (she called personally on a Sunday night to make sure the phone was working). Carol also contacted the local Chamber of Commerce and medical society to find out how her new customer could reach emergency medical services, and she referred the family to several local organizations, among them United Way, where special financial and emotional assistance was available for senior citizens.

For her actions, Carol was named a winner of her area's monthly "Count on Me" service accolades and was honored as the quarterly winner for the state.

The American Red Cross:
Paragon of Grace Under Fire

With its prodigious relief efforts for victims of natural as well as man-made disasters, the American Red Cross is perhaps the ultimate model for selfless—and often thankless—service to others under the most trying circumstances. The agency's volunteers routinely leave the comfort of home and family to work around the clock amidst the 90-mile-an-hour winds of hurricanes, the wreckage of earthquakes, threat of disease, and often the worry of rebel fire. These following examples of such life-and-limb acts are excerpted from the American Red Cross' web site.

Jennifer Brandewie, a young Navy wife and mother visiting her parents in Lexington, KY, was worried. She hadn't heard from her husband, Tim, an intelligence officer on a six-month mission aboard the U.S.S. Saipan, in weeks.

Then Jennifer got the scare of her life.

Tim finally called, but he could barely speak. The ship's doctor came on the line and told her that her husband had just had two emergency surgeries. Suddenly the line went dead—leaving Jennifer frantic.

"I didn't have a clue who to call," Jennifer says, "when my Mom suggested the Red Cross."

Kay Huff, an Armed Forces Emergency Service Coordinator at the Bluegrass Area Chapter, went straight into action. Working from the few facts the distraught wife could give her, it took 3 hours—and plenty of phone work—to gather the information they needed. Tim had been moved to a military hospital in Rota, Spain, and the Red Cross military station manager there forwarded Kay a doctor's statement and direct phone number so that Jennifer could speak with Tim and his doctor right away for updates on his situation.

"The Red Cross really came through for us," said Jennifer, back home in Virginia Beach, VA. "It was wonderful, because I was so worried and upset."

Kay's take on the episode exemplifies the Red Cross service ethic. "We feel a real responsibility here to help and reassure people like Jennifer."

"This is how I will die," Barbara Lindsay thought.

The wind roared, smashing glass and wood all around her home in Louisville, KY. She spotted her fifteen-year-old daughter near a far door in the house—the only door she couldn't get closed as the tornado hit. "I prayed, then reached out to her," Barbara says. "Suddenly the door slammed shut, and that end of the house caved in. The roof lifted off the back, and everything was sucked out of the rooms next to us." But her daughter was safe.

Barbara's home was one of 255 destroyed when a tornado struck suburban Louisville in May 1996. Within hours of the disaster, the entire metropolitan area rallied to help the victims, with the Louisville Chapter of the Red Cross leading the way.

When the noise stopped, Barbara opened the hall door and saw her house in shambles. "It's just so hard to believe that what you've worked for all your life is gone in 2 minutes," she says. But in no time, Red Cross volunteers had located her and given her and her three daughters the means to buy food, clothing, shoes, and household items. "And our children were able to talk to the Red Cross counselors about their fears," after the tornado,

she says. "The Red Cross was great—a godsend—because every little thing we had was gone."

In four months, with no little assistance from the Red Cross, Barbara had rebuilt her home and moved back in.

Like the other scouts of Troop 84, Mike Herdan was looking forward to the camping expedition in the remote wilderness of northern Minnesota.

The fifteen-year-old couldn't have known that he'd returned home hailed as a hero, thanks to his Red Cross training.

The trip started out well. The sixteen scouts from St. Joseph had pitched tents and bedded down. But their sleep was cut short before dawn by a freak storm packing 100-mile-per-hour winds. Trees began to topple, and the boys raced for their van.

They did a quick head count, and realized quickly that some of their members were missing. Assistant scoutmaster Chris Jaeger ran back to the campsite to find them, only to be pinned underneath a falling tree.

Luckily, Mike had completed Red Cross first aid training just 13 days earlier. He led the Scouts in stabilizing Chris so his extensive injuries wouldn't worsen. After using a tent pole to lift the 60-foot tree off Chris' broken leg, the boys put him on a makeshift cot, covered him with blankets, and carried him through underbrush and debris. "The cot kept getting stuck—only the adrenaline kept us going," says Mike.

The young rescuers trekked a mile before they reached others who'd been alerted to the emergency and were using chain saws to cut a path so Chris could be rushed to a hospital. He eventually recovered from multiple broken bones and head injuries.

Hospital staff noted that by being prepared, Mike not only had prevented further injury to Chris, he probably saved his friend's life—one of thousands saved every year by people who take health and safety courses from the Red Cross.

Another of the highly successful, but less publicized, services of Red Cross volunteers is "tracing," or tracking down relatives, friends, and others who've been lost track of or otherwise long since disappeared. It's led to some remarkable reunions.

Al Lovetro and Re Le Thuong met in 1971 during the Vietnam War. What started as a wartime romance developed into a solid, lasting relationship. Although the two had a child together and talked of getting married, Al was sent back to the United States alone after his tour of duty.

Back in the United States, Al worked hard to save enough money to bring Re Le and his son to America. He began looking forward to and planning the day of the big reunion. But not long after he had settled into his new life in the United States, Al was told by a fellow serviceman that Re Le and his son had been killed in Vietnam. Al was devastated. The photo he carried around of Re Le and his son in joyous hope suddenly became a painful reminder of a life that would not be.

But in June 1996, Al got a call from the American Red Cross with some startling news. Re Le and his son had not perished years earlier, but instead were in the United States and desperately wanted to be reacquainted. Re Le had filed a tracing request on Al at a Red Cross chapter two years earlier in Binghamton, NY.

With little information to go on and plenty of dead ends, the chapter caseworker finally was successful in finding Al. The caseworker had checked and rechecked with other Red Cross chapters around the country, until something finally turned up.

After reuniting and spending time together, Al and Re Le decided their separation had lasted far too long, and that November, Al moved to Binghamton to reunite with the woman and child he for so many years believed to be only a memory.

Excerpted from http://www.redcross.org

Breathing Life Into a Dying Dream

A few years ago Brooks and Ruth Bowen, co-owners of Travel Agents International in Richmond, VA, received a call from a local client who was hoping to fulfill a lifelong dream: to sail on the QE2 luxury ship round trip from New York to England. But there was a problem; the client had severe emphysema, and needed an oxygen tank with her at all times. It would be easy enough to fly the tanks via airline from Richmond to New York, the Bowens thought. The real challenge came in figuring out how to provide her with oxygen while she was on the ship for 11 days.

It wasn't quite so hard for Brooks and Ruth, however. They helped the client track down and order a mobile oxygen-producing machine she could pull around with her on board ship. "We finally got a hold of it, but it weighed 35 pounds and had to be taken with her on the plane," says Brooks. Due to her condition, the client wasn't able to carry anything substantial, let alone lug around the oxygen machine.

So, to make it possible for their client to take her dream trip—the last one before she passed away, it turned out later—Brooks and Ruth flew to and from New York with her, carried her oxygen tank and luggage on board, arranged the necessary help for her aboard the QE2, and made it possible for her to travel in ease, since she had no family willing or able to take care of her.

Contributed by Dick Landis

Never, Never, Never Quit

"Some people probably think I'm crazy to go to all the trouble I do sometimes, but I just think of the patient. What if that was my grandmother? I'd stand on my head and drink water if it would help."

Toni Omaits

As a referral testing specialist with SmithKline Beecham Clinical Laboratories in Tampa, FL, Toni Omaits links outside laboratories with medical clients who need highly specialized tests not routinely performed by most hospitals.

Her role as a troubleshooter sometimes requires that she go to extraordinary lengths for a customer, but nothing prepared her for the 10-hour saga she experienced a few years ago.

It started with a late afternoon request from one of the company's large hospital clients for an emergency gastric fluid test for an elderly woman. The woman was believed to have swallowed a poison. But only one test could determine that for certain.

Says Omaits, "I called just about everybody, but I didn't have any luck getting someone who could do the test." Eventually, she convinced a technologist at a Pennsylvania lab to personally perform the work—provided she could get him the specimen by midnight. Omaits made arrangements for one flight after another, only to see each delayed or canceled. As time ran out, she convinced airline employees to bend company policy and put the specimen on a flight that had already closed its doors and was readying for take-off.

Omaits contacted an airline employee on the receiving end and arranged to have the package rushed to a waiting taxi, which would deliver the sample to the technician.

The package arrived just minutes shy of his midnight deadline.

The situation was a rare one, Omaits says, but she wouldn't hesitate to go through it again. Speed, efficiency—and a genuine concern for the customer—are everything in her business, and she takes pride in delivering all three.

National Park Service Rangers to the Rescue

Think of our national parks and what comes to mind? Pristine beauty, rugged trails, turbulent rivers, deer, buffalo perhaps, even a roving grizzly or two. Our national parks are truly an irreplaceable treasure. Safeguarding these wonders of nature, and we the people who come to enjoy them, are the men and women of the National Park Service (NPS). The following tales of recent heroic rescues stand out to us as supreme examples of the resourcefulness and bold endurance of the do-whatever-it-takes NPS rangers.

Kathryn Byer and her husband decided to take advantage of a fine October day to hike a favorite trail in the Great Smoky Mountains in western North Carolina. Not long into the trip, Kathryn slipped and fell on some rocks lining Forney Creek. This was no minor tumble—she broke her ankle badly in the fall. After tending to and stabilizing Kathy, her husband hiked to find a park ranger and get some much-needed help. It was getting dark, and Kathy was worried both about her husband—who had been gone what seemed like forever—and her own painful condition. A few hours later, Ranger Glenn Martin arrived, placed Kathy's ankle in a splint, and began to, in Kathy's words, "Prepare me for what would prove to be a daunting and dangerous rescue mission. I was told it would take 15 to 20 rangers to carry me out, and that most of the rescue would have to be done in the dark, taking 3 hours or more.

"She began to wonder why any ranger, let alone 15 to 20 of them, would want to put personal safety at risk to try to carry her uphill for 3 miles to the Clingman's Dome parking lot. Especially with all the recent trail washouts and other trail deterioration.

These rangers would have to be pretty brave, she decided. And she was right. "Over the next several hours I had the privilege of witnessing some of the most heroic men and women I've ever met. By the time we arrived back at Clingman's Dome, most of my rescuers were totally exhausted. It had taken us not 3 hours, but nearly 5 hours to get out."

In a letter to Great Smoky Superintendent Karen Wade following the rescue, Kathryn wrote:

I would like to make this letter one of thanks for and celebration of these people. I know only a few names—Glenn, Allison, Betty—but over the nearly 5 hours I was strapped in the litter, I came to know all of their faces, and their voices, well. `Your federal government at work,' one of the younger men joked, as they hoisted me over yet another large rock. Yes, indeed, and I, for one, am thankful for that work. My husband and I have always loved this park; now we have a deeply personal reason for that love. As soon as I am able to hike again, probably not till next spring, I plan to come back, and I intend to keep coming back for as long as I live.

Marlys Weber and friend Ronald Hannula of Minneapolis, MN, had finally decided to take their long-awaited adventure to Isle Royale, an island in Lake Superior, and one of the most remote and rugged parcels in the National Park Service. How remote? It's about a 5-hour ferry boat ride from the Upper Peninsula of Michigan, and humans are only temporary visitors for a short time each year. Come winter, Isle Royale is the only national park to completely close down. It's also one of the last places you'd want to encounter any serious physical problems.

But that's exactly what happened when Hannula suffered a debilitating stroke while hiking the island's back-country.

The stroke launched a tortuous and protracted 10-hour evacuation to get Hannula the proper medical attention. It involved a 3-mile carryout of Hannula over narrow trails by NPS rangers, a boat transport, and then a helicopter trip back to a Marquette, Michigan hospital.

That's tough enough to pull off in broad daylight, yet the entire rescue happened in the blackness of night.

Here's part of the letter Hannula's friend Marlys wrote to Isle Royale headquarters in the rescue's aftermath:

I find words inadequate to thank you and your staff for the heroic care and concern toward my partner Ron and your graciousness to me while "marooned" on Mott Island (site of park administrative headquarters). By Friday, August 23, we knew that Ron's left carotid artery was 100% occluded and right carotid artery 95% occluded and ulcerated—the cause of his stroke. Too much at risk for surgery, he was flown home from Marquette General Hospital on drugs to thin his blood. He will have surgery in 4 weeks.

We are both grateful for the unbelievable effort and journey your staff made, and also the wonderful volunteers who pitched in. Without all of your help, Ron may not have survived. As upset as I was when the helicopter flew away with Ron and without me, I will always treasure my experiences on Mott Island, and the hospitable and friendly people I met there.

Contributed by John Quinley

6

Memorable People

Some people are memorable through the sheer dint of their personalities; others by the strength of their words and deeds. Still others linger in the mind because of the gracious and graceful manner in which they seem always to conduct themselves—they are a pleasure to witness in action. The most memorable of the memorable seem to combine a bit of all three. John F. Kennedy and Martin Luther King, Jr., were men of vivid personality, high purpose, eloquent speech, and involvement. Mother Teresa is the symbol of dogged determination, single minded focus, grace, and humility.

Not all memorable people play their lives out on such a grand stage. There was that third-grade teacher who you could never forget. She made learning fun and interesting and important to you for the first time.

There was the boss who said you had a talent for this kind of work, and who thanked you for your efforts and took a genuine interest in your development. He really made you feel that you were doing an important job and doing it well.

And then there was Jane—or John or Cathy or Miguel—that standout colleague with nary a phony bone in his or her body, a model of how you make customers—the good, the bad, and the ugly alike—feel great about being customers. And she or he was equally skilled at making you feel special and talented by mentoring and coaching you through the hard spots.

Perhaps what makes these people most memorable is their level of caring—they care about what they do, the people they do it for, and the people they do it along side of, with remarkable and inspiring consistency.

They care that their customers are pleased, that their co-workers are happy, and that everyone they come in contact with is a little better for it.

What follows are stories of six memorable customer service people. People we—and others—have come in contact with and been so impressed by, that we—and they—have just had to let the world in on their feats and unique spirit.

Jeff Amland: Rain and Snow and Dark of Night Keep This Partnership on Course

Late Thanksgiving Eve Jeff Amland called. "I've been listening to the weather forecasts all day," he began, "and it sounds like there's gonna be 3 to 6 inches of snow on the ground by morning. Is there any specific time you need your driveway open tomorrow?"

There wasn't.

He persisted, "Don't you have out of town people coming?"

They'd already arrived, and since we'd been hearing the same weather predictions as Jeff, we had planned accordingly. We weren't going anywhere but down the lane and back, and even that on foot, or at our most ambitious, via cross-country skis.

"Well, I'll put you down for afternoon then. But if you change your mind, call me at the shop. I'll be working on the plows for another couple of hours anyway."

Thanksgiving morning, around 11:00 A.M., Jeff called again.

"I'll have you plowed out by three if that's still okay."

We'd already been out on foot, and even though the village plow had thrown a couple of feet across the mouth of the drive, we could easily push our way out to the highway in an emergency.

"Let me give you the number for the truck phone just in case."

Two years earlier, we hired Jeff, a.k.a. AAgro-GREEN Professional Lawn Services, to come plow us out from under a freak 20-inch Thanksgiving snowstorm—the second such storm of the year. It was an act of blind desperation. Our regular snow plowing guy had gone on vacation, and at 6 P.M. Thanksgiving Day plus 1, his designated emergency backup was impatiently explaining to me that he had a family he hadn't seen since 4 A.M. the previous day. Didn't I think, he bleated, that he and his deserved to celebrate the holiday weekend too? We gave him 2 hours to change his mind. He didn't. We called Jeff.

We didn't know Jeff from a post, as we say here in the upper Midwest. But Jeff's flyer had been there in the accordion file we use for household bills and receipts, supermarket coupons, car and boat titles, canceled checks, and appliance warranties. A mail box stuffer we'd kept for no clear reason other than just-in-case. So I gave him a call.

"I have your snow removal brochure. I know you're probably swamped, but we have a family member with a medical condition, we have relatives we're going to have to get to the airport tomorrow, and I can't find anyone willing to plow us out in less than 2 days."

"Has the village cleared the main road yet?" he asked.

It had—leaving a 6-foot wall of ice and snow at the bottom of the hill in the process.

"Have you marked the sides?"

I had, with four foot orange stakes.

"Are you lit at night?"

We are and were.

"I have two regular customers between where I am right now and where you are. So would 8:30 tonight be soon enough?"

By 9:15 that evening we had a clear path to the main road— and the relieved feeling that we could deliver our charges to the airport the next morning safely and on time. And AAgroGREEN had a new customer.

That all transpired in November 1991. In mid-April 1992, generally the end of the snow-fall season here in Minnesota, Jeff stopped by with a bottle of wine. "Just a little thank you for your business and for recommending me to so many of your neighbors." We had, gladly, and with no prompting.

"Did you get my note about maybe doing your lawn work this year?"

Jeff's "note" was a detailed assessment of the condition of our lawn—as much as the thaw had exposed, anyway—and a proposal for remedying the same. It included the dates he thought the lawn should be thatched and fertilized and reseeded; the materials he felt would be appropriate to the job, and what he thought a reasonable mowing, edging, and weed treatment schedule might look like. He also included information on how he would pick a start date and what he would do to put the lawn to bed in the fall. And the price, while not the lowest we'd ever seen on an estimate, was well within the competitive range.

Over the past six winters and summers, we've actually seen Jeff and crew working on our place just eight or 10 times. In winter, he plows after we've left for work—our arrangement, except for those rare occasions when nature visits us with a foot or more of snow in 24 hours—and in summer he mows and fertilizes and sprays and harvests the dandelion crop before we're back home in the evening.

But we always know he's been there from the work—and from the notes. When he fertilizes and sprays he leaves a note detailing the chemicals and what-not he's used, along with a suggested watering schedule for the next few days. Last winter he clipped the top off an ornamental driveway light. The note recounted the damage—damage I wouldn't have found on my own until spring, if at all—and asked me if there was someplace special I'd like him to purchase the replacement, and to leave any special instructions for the reinstallation.

When Jeff adds a new person to his lawn care or snow removal crew he brings him around in the evening and introduces him. "I'd hate for you to come home some day and find a stranger working on your property," he explains.

Then there are the little things he does just because he thinks they need doing and because "I just thought you might get a kick out of it." One evening last winter we arrived home unusually early and caught Jeff in the act of finishing up the driveway. Badly in need of a little fresh air and exercise, Susan and I did the walks and the upper apron of the driveway, while Jeff concentrated on de-icing the slippery crest of our 30 degree drive. When the bill for that day arrived, he had deducted ten dollars from the usual total for, in his words, "removal assistance."

Last fall the warm weather lingered an unusually long time, and as a consequence leaf removal in the neighborhood moved at a rather leisurely pace. Particularly in our yard. When the weather took a sudden turn to the more normal, that is, became bitterly cold and blustery, Jeff rounded up a crew and canvassed his accounts to remove leaves where they had been allowed to languish, and even moved lawn furniture to shelter for those of us who were irrationally holding out hope for one more weekend of fun in the Fall sun. Of course none of that work ever appeared on an invoice.

Jeff knows—whether by intuition or from trial-and-error experience—two important things. The first is the value of keeping a customer, if not for life, for a long, long time. The second, that keeping customers for a long, long time means never taking them for granted, and never believing that there isn't yet another interesting way to let your actions tell your customers you care about their business.

Ron Zemke

Lorinda Evans Tucker: The Stick-to-It Secretary

That Friday morning in August put Lorinda Evans Tucker to the test. The phone call from Macon, GA to the Louisville, KY offices of H.B. Fuller was from a frantic occasional customer in desperate need of help. This customer, it seems, was running out of the glue it required for a specialized manufacturing operation. This particular glue, it turned out, wasn't one of the products it bought from Lorinda's company, but the caller was desperate.

The prospects were bleaker than the customer knew: this particular morning, Lorinda's boss, the VP of sales, was out of the country, and the local salesman was on vacation. Time to take a message, right? Not in Tucker's view. She called the company's regional technical service center in Greensboro, NC, and described the problem. Someone there determined which of the related glues among H.B. Fuller's 7,000 adhesive, sealant, and coating formulations would probably do the job. Then he lobbed the ball back into her court: the only stock on hand was in Louisville, KY. Not at all daunted, Tucker walked out of the office, drove her own pickup to the warehouse, loaded up 500 pounds of product, and headed for the airport. Elapsed time: 90 minutes so far.

At the airport, she encountered another hurdle. A big one. The air freight company that linked Louisville and Macon had a flight scheduled to leave in 30 minutes, but her employer didn't have an account with it. The bill was going to be pretty close to $300.00, and the freighter wasn't about to accept good intentions in lieu of cash on the counter. Back in a minute, guys. Tucker raced her pickup to the main terminal of the Louisville airport, found a handy automatic teller machine, and withdrew the money needed from her personal savings. By 2 P.M., the material was in Macon, the manufacturer's production system was not just running uninterrupted, but was operating better than ever (the new adhesive outperformed the one they'd been buying from the other supplier), and Tucker was back in the office.

So why had Tucker gone through so much on a sultry August morning for a customer who wasn't even using a Fuller Product?

In her words, "When the phone rings, it's your customer. And you do what you can to help them until you can find someone who can help them better. On that particular day, no one was in a better position to help them than I was."

And that occasional customer? Today it's a multimillion dollar H.B. Fuller customer.

Kristin Anderson

Penny Nirider Has an Unusual View:
She Likes Her Customers

Thomas Petzinger, Jr., writes "The Front Lines" column for the
Wall Street Journal. His profiles of small business people and unusual entrepreneurs have become a must read for millions.
Among our favorites is this one, about accountant turned mail
order mavin Penny Nirider.

Her success sprang from a blizzard, a football game, and a
talk show. But mostly it came from her instinct for putting herself in her customers' shoes.

Penny Nirider, 36 years old, is a whiz with a spreadsheet.
Even in Thorntown, IN, a town of but 3,000, she found plenty of
work helping companies computerize accounts. Because she had
two small boys, she worked from her home, usually between 9
P.M. and 2 A.M.

About three years ago, with the boys starting school, she
took a day job handling accounts payable for a company called
Enduron. Enduron employed fifty-five people bending metal for
Indiana's bustling travel-trailer industry. Automating the company made a huge difference on the bottom line, prompting the
owners eventually to make Ms. Nirider a partner.

Metal-bending is a volatile business, so the company decided to diversify by purchasing a little plastics shop called Wilmarc. With just five employees, Wilmarc made composting bins, leaf baggers, and an unusual rounded shovel that scraped away snow without bending or lifting. They called it Snow-Ease.

Ms. Nirider, given charge of the unit, discovered that running a small plastics business was nothing like running a spreadsheet. Wilmarc sold to hardware distributors, an industry she knew nothing about. There were uniform sales agreements. She also sensed some hardware people didn't take her seriously because she was female.

Then one day shortly before last Christmas, an elderly woman phoned Wilmarc headquarters. The caller owned a Snow-Ease but wanted another and couldn't find one. Would the factory ship one?

Wilmarc had never sold directly to a customer. Indeed, each Snow-Ease folded into a feeble box designed for retail display, and Wilmarc shipped these strictly by the case. For all Ms. Nirider knew, distribution agreements prohibited selling at retail. But the caller was so sweet and seemed so needful! So a Snow-Ease carton was dispatched to Pittsburgh for $19.95, or $10.00 below retail.

Just after Christmas, a big snow hit the East. Lynn Cullen, the host of a popular morning talk show on Pittsburgh's WTAE, told her listeners that some miscreant had stolen her snow shovel. Later, off the air, Cullen heard from the elderly woman, who said she could solve her snow woes with a call to Indiana. When the call came, Nirider again could not say no.

A few days later, an employee named Monica Taylor opened up Wilmarc's cinder-block office to find the phone already ringing. It was a third Pittsburgher seeking a Snow-Ease. The instant she hung up, another call came in, also from Pittsburgh, then another and another. It was a stunt, she figured; the Pittsburgh Steelers were facing the Indianapolis Colts a week later in the playoffs. But soon it became obvious that the Pittsburgh radio personality was raving about the Snow-Ease and had given out Wilmar's number over the air.

Unfortunately, she had also said the Snow-Ease sold for just $19.95.

Nirider agonized. Shipping boxes one at a time would be unprofitable and might upset distributors. But the Pittsburgh callers were buried in snow. And whoever was at fault for the price confusion, it certainly wasn't the callers.

"We didn't have a clue what we were doing," Nirider says. "But I knew what I would expect as a customer." So $19.95 it was.

There was yet another dilemma. Never having sold at retail, Wilmarc wasn't a credit-card merchant. But in a snow emergency, how could the company expect people to pay in advance? So Nirider shipped the product with invoices to follow. "It was just common courtesy," she says. (Barely 1% defaulted.)

As the orders rolled in, Nirider realized she was having more fun than she had ever enjoyed in business. Partly it was the escalating banter with callers over the approaching Colts-Steelers game. (The Steelers won, forcing Nirider to pay up on a few long-distance bets.) Everybody was so easygoing. Her gender, moreover, didn't matter. Dealing with the public, she found, "You get to be yourself. You don't have to play any games."

Unhappily, of course, the more she sold, the more she lost. With orders unabating after two weeks, she needed an honorable way out. So Wilmarc purchased ads on WTAE notifying people that several days hence, on January 31, 1996, the company would begin charging the established retail price of $29.95.

Even at that price the orders flew in. Nirider noticed that they were soon coming from Ohio and West Virginia, thanks to word-of-mouth. By April, Wilmarc had sold 2,100 Snow-Ease shovels directly to consumers across the region, many times the number it sold through the usual distributors, none of whom complained.

Today, Wilmarc has a separate retail mail-order business. Nirider is hoping for 6,000 retail Snow-Ease orders this winter. If word-of-mouth continues to multiply at the rate of last year, she figures the Snow-Ease may one day be ready for national promotion.

So if you ever see an advertisement for the Snow-Ease, I hope you'll recall the lesson of Penny Nirider: Every person who contacts your business—every elderly lady, every talk show host, every football fan—stands at the beginning of a long line of potential customers. Resolve dilemmas in their favor and they'll return to you more than you had to give away.

Al Cole: Cabbie on the Climb

Al Cole's business card says: "Call for the Pro." Al is a cab driver for United Cab of Houston, TX, and he is a pro. Maybe even the pro's pro.

A few weeks ago, I happened into Al's cab at the Houston airport en route to an after dinner talk at the Woodlands Conference Center, a few miles north of Houston. Al was pleasant enough, hardly one of those "Chatty Charlie" cabbies, either. He likes driving a cab, he says, and is saving his pennies to take a crack at restaurant management—his own—someday.

A few minutes before we reached the conference center, Al made a perfunctory inquiry about my plans for returning to the airport the next day. I had told him I was just doing an in-and-out, so he smelled the possibility of a good first fare the next day.

I allowed as to how my host had probably taken care of that, but if he hadn't, I knew the conference center had an airport service. "Great," said Al, adding, "I'm sure everything will be just fine, but let me offer some advice, if I may, on early morning traffic going into Houston from out here. I live out here myself, and frankly, it's awful. There was an accident on I-95 just this morn-

I used to drive a cab. Now, I'm into taxi service.

ing that had traffic tied up for two hours. Be sure that whoever takes you to the airport starts out an hour to an hour and a half before your flight. You never know."

And for good measure he gave me his blue-on-blue business card along with his home and car phone numbers. "If you find out that your ride is a problem, just call me," he said. "I'll be in the cab until eight, and at home after that. Call anytime. By the way, which airport?"

"Which airport?" I asked, not aware that I had options.

"There are two, International and Hobby," he said. I checked my ticket, it was Hobby. "That's further. Definitely leave yourself the hour and a half."

As fate would have it, my ride turned out to be more problematic than I thought. The volunteer who was going to drive me to the airport was a no-show, and the conference center's airport shuttle made its first run about the same time as my homeward-bound flight left the ground. So I called Al.

"Great, see you at 6:15 A.M., Mr. Zemke, and I'll bring the coffee," he said cheerily.

The phone rang the next morning at 5:50 A.M. "Mr. Zemke, this is Al Cole from United Cab," the call began, as thoughts of "Oh God, he's not coming!" ran through my head. A worried sounding "Yes?" was all I mustered.

"I'm here a little early," Al said. "The weather report last night was for fog, and sure enough it's foggy on the road. I just thought I'd better get over here a little early, just in case. Do you want me to drive over to your lodge or shall I wait out front?"

Persuaded by Al's tactful wake-up call, I reported to the front door of the conference center, bags in hand, promptly at 6:05 A.M. And true to his word—better in fact—Al was there with not only hot coffee, but a newspaper and tasty Danish as well.

As we flew down the highway toward Houston's Hobby Airport, Al kept up a stream of CB chatter with other early-bird cabbies about traffic conditions on the road ahead. In the odd dull moment, he waxed hopeful again about owning his own business and asked my opinion about a variety of opportunities from fast-food franchises to office equipment repair.

Traffic was lighter than anticipated, and we hit the "For Passenger Discharge and Pick Up Only" area with 45 minutes to spare. Al proceeded to serve up directions to and give reviews of all the breakfast bars in the airport. I offered breakfast on me in return for the super service.

"Thanks but no thanks," he replied, "I got a good feeling about today. If I really hit it, I can get that business of my own started just that much sooner."

Given the samples of work ethic and service sense I'd been exposed to in the past 18 hours, I wouldn't bet against him. And the next time I hear some corporate hothouse type saying something like "people don't want to work today," or "they" (meaning those frontline folks) don't really understand what good service is," I'm going to be sorely tempted to whip out Al's little blue-on-blue business card and recommend they take not a long walk on a short pier, but a fast ride on a foggy freeway in Houston.

Ron Zemke

Alan Wilk: A Passion for Clogged Drains— and Customers

Len Schlesinger is a professor at the Harvard Business School. His research and writings on the economics of customer care and making quality service a competitive strategy, are widely known and respected. But Schlesinger, who was an executive with the Au Bon Pain restaurant chain in the 1980s, knows that great customer service isn't really just formulas and corporate strategy. He knows full well that memorable, "knock your socks off" customer service is about sweat and effort and winning the right to serve, one customer at a time. And really liking what you are doing.

As a reminder to managers that quality service is a frontline game, he co-authored a wonderful book called, *The Real Heroes of Business... and Not A CEO Among Them* (Currency Double-day, 1994), which chronicles the exploits of fourteen highly memorable customer service heroes. Our favorite is Alan Wilk, a Roto-Rooter employee with a passion for cleaning the most stubborn drains and sewers in New York City; a man Schlesinger calls "a one-man rescue squad." The following is Schlesinger's profile of Wilk, abridged.

There are a million clogged drains in the naked city, and one man can clean them all.

When Alan Wilk showed up at Charlie Mihulka's house in the Glendale section of Queens one winter night in 1985, his chances of success seemed remote. The pipe connecting Mihulka's house to the main sewer was plugged, and four sewer and drain companies had come out over several days, each cockier than the last, only to be defeated by the pipe. They left behind

plenty of advice—a couple of them said only an expensive, high pressure jet truck could clear the clog, one told Mihulka the pipe was broken and had to be dug up and replaced—and they left behind their bills.

It was just the kind of situation Wilk relishes: an exasperated customer and a devilishly difficult pipe for an opponent—a pipe that had already amassed an unbeaten 4-0 record against the professional pipe cleaners. Now it was time for Alan Wilk of Roto-Rooter to step up to the sewer trap.

Alan Wilk almost never meets a pipe problem he can't solve. His way with balky plumbing is second only to his ability to calm the people who are being victimized by their pipes and drains. The pipe was indeed a nasty one. Working in the basement, Alan was eventually able to determine—mostly by the noises his snake made as it traveled down the pipe—that it had a deep sag in it. The ground had settled beneath his pipe, giving it a broad V-shape as it carried its cargo from the house in the sewer main running beneath the street. In the bottom of the V had collected what Alan describes as "sludge—stuff the consistency of oatmeal and tar."

The problem, Alan decided, was simple: the sludge was blocking the pipe, but all the multibladed head on his snake did was slice through the sludge, it didn't clear it away. The snake's tip—which looks like a combination of a hand-mixer and a food processor blade—was designed to cut away root blockages (hence "Roto-Rooter") and solidified clogs. It was all but useless against the sludge.

Alan pondered the problem—not unlike a surgeon contemplating a badly clogged artery—and conceived a new technique. "Technique sometimes gets you more than brute strength." he says. From the ample stock of implements in his customized van, Alan picked a wire-brush disk, which he attached to the end of the snake. The spinning disk would present a nearly solid face to the sludge. With a little help from water pumped into the pipe to make things flow out in the right direction, the spinning wire brush whisked the tarry sludge right out of the pipe. Who needed a jet truck, at $600 per visit? Who needed a new pipe, at $2,000 a throw? All Charlie Milhulka needed was Alan Wilk.

Alan Wilk is a drain cleaning genius constantly searching for less costly, more convenient ways to do everything. Take his flashlights, for instance. A Roto-Rooter man, constantly peering under sinks, into drains, and at angles of old plumbing, needs reliable, powerful flashlights, and can spend a fair sum keeping them supplied with batteries. The flashlight problem didn't occupy Alan Wilk very long. He strapped a car headlight to a motorcycle battery, and he had a better flashlight than he could ever buy. He's wired up his van with two big truck batteries and appropriate electrical outlets—both alternate current and direct current—and he just plugs in his flashlights between calls and charges them as he drives around the city.

Alan's truck is kind of an oversized Swiss Army knife on wheels. Behind the passenger seat, he has rigged up a glove dryer using an old car air conditioning blower and some plastic pipe punched with holes. The gloves fit over the pipes, and the blower forces air through the pipes and through the gloves. Alan rarely has to endure the discomfort of pulling on a pair of cold, wet work gloves.

Alan's improvements are everywhere. He's even got huge street maps of New York City mounted on window shade rods over the windshield on the driver's side in his truck. At stoplights, he can pull a map down, consult it, and when the light turns green, one tug and the map disappears.

Alan Wilk is also a student of human behavior, which he has occasion to observe routinely at what is often a time of surprise, frustration, and disgust: the moments after the toilet overflows.

Alan, for instance, never goes to the bathroom in his customers' homes. He perceives something most other workers—plumbers, painters, exterminators—either ignore or overlook: customers don't want him to.

"Some people feel really funny about that," he says. "Most people, if they don't like it, they wouldn't say no. But I don't want to impose on anybody. It's not a policy of the company's, it's just sensitivity. Rather than put somebody on the spot..." And in fact, most people are slightly put off at the prospect of strangers using their bathrooms.

It's not a problem for Alan, he's rigged up a urinal in the back corner of his truck. It's next to the handwashing station, and the shower.

Alan is a cheerful man by nature, and determined, and he usually figures that time is on his side. A challenging problem makes him more determined, and frequently more cheerful. As the hours—and the snakes—unspool without success, most people would get progressively more pessimistic and discouraged. Alan simply senses victory getting closer and closer.

"I come in and you're in a tizzy," he said. "I will not leave you till everything's working properly and back in order. Relax. It's like Allstate: you're in good hands."

Alan doesn't hurry—unless he senses that you want him to finish and get out. Although Alan and all his fellow Roto-Rooter service people work strictly on commission—between 30 and 40 percent of each job—you would never guess it from his manner.

"The first thing I do in a house is smile," he says. "That's hokey, I know. But I'm a hokey guy. And a sincere smile seems to relax people."

He gives no sense of being antsy to get one job over with so he can race to the next one—although theoretically, the faster he works, the more jobs he does, the more money he makes. Alan often takes the time to do a little more than he's actually asked, and he always cleans up after himself—trying to make no mess at all, and often leaving the basement or bathroom where he's working far less wet and smelly than he finds it.

What is truly amazing, given his unhurried approach, is that most years Alan Wilk is one of the most productive, and therefore one of the highest paid, Roto-Rooter men in New York City. Many years he earns $70,000 or more, and says of his customers, "I enjoy seeing the look on people's faces when they realize they're not being taken advantage of."

At fifty years old, Alan Wilk has in fact achieved a complete state of grace as a Roto-Rooter man. He loves the work, he loves the people, and he still marvels at his luck in stumbling into exactly the right job.

"I've been doing this 16 years, it fits me to a tee," he says "I see a problem, I diagnose the problem, I solve the problem. People are happy to see you."

In a different universe, Alan might have had the opportunity to go to college and become a scientist or an engineer or a surgeon. But he has no regrets.

"If I'd gone to college," he says, "I might not have found this."

Patti Schutta: Always Time for That Little Extra Service

Patti Schutta serves walk-in customers for Minnegasco, a Minneapolis, MN, based subsidiary of NorAm Energy Corp., at the company's downtown Minneapolis convenience center. And though customers can pay bills by mail and solve problems over the telephone, Patti has developed a loyal following at the center. Customers, predominantly seniors, who wouldn't feel right if they didn't come to Patti's office to sit and chat for a moment, and carefully count out their payments in cash from marked budget minder envelopes, are frequent visitors.

Patti has gotten to know Walter and Agnes Pearson pretty well. They are getting on in years, and Agnes is not well. Nonetheless, or perhaps because of her health, Walter tells Patti, he wouldn't think of leaving her alone at home when it comes time to venture out to pay the bills. So—rain or shine, snow or swelter—once a month the devoted couple bundle up, board a bus, and venture out to meet their obligations. Their route never varies. First they pay their electric bill at Northern States Power (NSP) Company's downtown office, then they visit Patti to take care of the gas.

The weather in Minneapolis in February hardly rivals Miami or Phoenix for creature comfort, but the 18th was at least sunny and a few degrees above zero; an altogether "pleasant" day by mid-winter Minnesota standards. But it wasn't a very nice day by Walter and Agnes' standards. The Pearson's utility bills were all out of whack, and Walter was thoroughly con-

fused. NSP, the power company, which had been Walter and Agnes' first stop, had told Walter he'd made a mistake and his bill was a mess—and their explanation had gone right over his head.

Frustrated and cowed by his NSP problem, Walter unloaded his concerns on his Minnegasco connection. Patti sifted through Walter's careful, handwritten records looking for clues. In a matter of minutes, she discovered the problem: Walter had copied readings from his gas meter onto his electric company meter card. She assured him that it was a reasonable mistake—and there was no reason to be hard on himself. And when Patti offered to untangle the mess, Walter was more than a little relieved.

Patti picked up the phone, called her counterpart at the power company and explained what she'd figured out *with* the Pearsons. As they talked, Patti learned that it had actually been several years since the Pearson's electric meter had actually been read, and that the Pearson's bills were actually estimates. So, checking Walter and Agnes' availability, she made an appointment for the coming Friday and wrote a note on the top of her calendar on the page marked the 21st: "CALL WALTER—REMIND HIM NSP IS COMING."

As Patti carefully explained the purpose of the meter reading house call and wrote down instructions, she realized that Agnes couldn't see the paper on the desk, and asked Agnes what had happened to her glasses. "They're broken," Walter said, and added that after all they'd been through, he wasn't going to go to the optical place to get them fixed today as they'd planned. He'd had enough for this day. She'd just have to wait until next time, Walter said. Agnes was tired too, so she didn't protest too much.

Patti, however, was uncomfortable leaving Agnes in a blur until Walter was ready to venture out again. "Is the prescription in your glasses still good?" "Yes," Agnes allowed, "it is." "So you just need the frames repaired?" "Yes," Agnes confirmed, "that would solve the problem."

"Good," concluded Patti, "Would it be okay with you if I had them repaired and delivered?" Taken aback, the Pearsons nonetheless gratefully accepted Patti's offer.

Later that afternoon Patti used her break to deliver the glasses to a nearby optical store. "Two days, no problem," the optician pronounced. Back at the office Patti and her boss Bev worked out a strategy. Bev's job included calling on businesses in the community and she could indeed drop Agnes' glasses off between appointments.

An awful lot of trouble for a small-change residential customer? Sure. But to Patti Schutta, there are no unimportant customers, just customers with different-sized needs.

"After all," she says," No one's problems are inconsequential—to them."

Contributed by Karen Miller

7
Keeping Great Company

Giving great service is contagious.

There are some companies—and associations and governmental departments as well—where that contagion is the equivalent of a year-round viral outbreak, a kind of customer-focused flu bug that gleefully infects everyone in the organization.

In these organizations there is a commitment to customers that goes beyond the frontline effort into the very heart of the operation. There are structures and principles and values that make it expressly essential that the needs and expectations of customers come first. Sometimes adhering to that focus is natural and easy; a walk in the park. Other times it takes a dig-down-deep, tighten-the-belt, find-something-extra effort. It is the latter that tests the mettle of both individuals and organizations. And it is the difference between organizations whose customers sing their praises and come back again and again—and those whose customers simply feel that, "they're not any worse than anybody else," and sometimes come back and sometimes don't.

The six companies profiled in this chapter excel in two important ways: they make their companies "easy-to-do-business-with" and they're masters at creative, responsive service recovery. They delight in doing the little things that make day-to-day dealings with them just a bit more memorable for customers than doing business with those "other guys."

Are the six organizations profiled here perfect? No, probably not. Do they make mistakes? Undoubtedly. Do they disappoint some customers? Yes, occasionally. But they refuse to believe that bad things just inevitably have to happen to some of their customers.

Several years ago we listened in rapt fascination as James Barksdale, now CEO of NetScape Communication Corp. but then COO of Federal Express Corp., apologized to a group of executives at a quality conference for the fact that FedEx's guaranteed overnight delivery service was on-time "only" 98 percent of the time. Several of the assembled snickered a bit at that declaration. Undaunted, Barksdale continued, "If we have 98 percent overnight delivery of 800,000 packages and letters, then 16,000—2 percent—of our customers did not receive their package absolutely, positively, overnight. I'm not inclined to brag too loudly about 16,000 packages gone astray."

That's the attitude and mind-set that distinguish and motivate people in these organizations—and organizations like them—that are known not only for the meritorious efforts of a few scattered individuals, but for consistent, widespread, every-one-in-the-same-boat service excellence.

Norwest Bank: Where Customers Are at the Heart of Service

Norwest Bank is no mom and pop operation. It offers community banking through more than 800 branches in 16 states, has 53,000 employees and $80 billion in assets. And employees believe passionately in retail banking and customer service. Which, according to the *Wall Street Journal*, makes Norwest pretty unique.

> "Most bankers consider retail branches so expensive that they should be replaced by automated teller machines and `home banking,' the *Wall Street Journal* writes. Personal service, they believe, must be reserved for the affluent. Norwest Corp. has another idea. It actually encourages visits by the less-than-affluent, offering free coffee and cookies to senior citizens the day Social Security checks are issued." (WSJ, August 17, 1995)

Richard Kovacevich, CEO of the Minneapolis-headquartered company, doesn't believe that long-term success for Norwest rests purely in products like home banking, complex investment instruments, or `smart' cards. Nor does he believe in charging customers for the privilege of talking to a teller, or forcing them to use ATMs so he can cut labor costs. He believes the bank's success now, and in the future, depends upon having the products customers need and providing service that makes them comfortable and happy that they've chosen Norwest to be their financial services company.

What does great service—called *Service to the Nth Degree*® at the bank—look like? It has many faces.

In Mesa, AZ, Tim Huish received a phone call from a man who needed a document notarized. The man, a double amputee, had called Huish's branch of Norwest in desperation. He was, in fact a customer of a different bank and had just been told that he'd have to bring the document to the bank to have it notarized—the bank didn't make house calls. Huish and Theresa Holmes, another Mesa Norwest employee, drove to the man's home, did the notarization, and ensured the man's documents were headed off to their proper destination. Any guesses where the man decided to re-house his bank accounts?

When Steve Reed of Fox Valley, WI, learned that a small business owner—a prospective employee benefits plan customer—was having trouble interesting his employees in attending an off-hours meeting to learn about the plan, Reed didn't bat an eye. He and his fellow Norwest employees arranged and personally catered a mid-day picnic lunch in a local park for the group. Three hundred employees and their spouses turned out for the eats and information.

Sometimes great service is a matter of not taking `No' for an answer. Gene Eike and Sue Johnson, who work in Norwest banking stores in Stillwater and Woodbury, MN, thought they had devised a mortgage, home equity, and personal loan package a customer couldn't resist. But the couple didn't show up for the closing. A call determined that a competitor had made an attractive counteroffer. Undeterred, Eike went to the customers'

home, learned what the competitor had offered and called colleague Johnson. Three visits later, the determined duo had arranged to payoff the customers' line of credit, refinance their home mortgage, and converted them to the bank's checking, savings, and credit card services as well. The net result: a new customer for Norwest, and a customer whose finances were back on sound footing.

In Billings, MT, Norwest teller Lisa Fricks saw a story in the local paper about a homeless man who was robbed and assaulted twice in less than a week. While others in the community looked into housing for the man, Fricks arranged a free checking and savings account for him and set up direct deposit authorization for his Social Security and Supplemental Security Income payments.

The Norwest Nth Degree® ethic works because it is a top-to-bottom ethic. An Arizona customer discovered that first hand when she found herself on the outside of a branch looking in after arriving past bank hours. The woman was desperate. She needed a cashier's check to close escrow on her new house. A passerby asked her why she looked so forlorn. She told him her story, he knocked on the bank's glass door and gestured a teller over. The teller opened the door, wrote the check, and the woman made her closing deadline. Only later did she learn that the Samaritan was Jon Campbell, president and CEO of Norwest Bank Arizona.

A question that comes naturally to mind is, how does this big time, small-town bank perform financially? Is it simply a marginally performing dinosaur waiting to be gobbled by a smarter, faster, cost-cutting competitor? Not according to the balance sheet. Norwest has grown revenues 20 percent a year since 1988, and in 1995 its return on equity, reports the *Wall Street Journal*, "exceeded that of almost all of the nation's biggest, best-regarded banks."

Contributed by Jill Packey

H.E. Butt Grocery Stores: Where Great Service Is in the Bag

You don't often hear "great service" and "grocery store" in the same sentence. Sure, there was the mom and pop corner grocery of your childhood days where the owners knew your name and gave you free penny candies from time to time. And there is fabled Stew Leonard's Dairy in Norwalk, CT, that features clowns and a mechanical band, and people in chicken and cow costumes—and service so good they made a movie about it. But by and large, ever since Clarence Sanders opened the first modern supermarket in 1916 at 79 Jefferson Street, Memphis, TN, grocery stores have been about efficiency and price, not service and civility.

Family-owned H-E-B Grocery tries hard to be an exception to that rule. It's a big task for a big company. Founded in a presupermarket era as "Mrs. C.C. Butt's Staple and Fancy Groceries" in 1905 in the Texas hill country town of Kerrville, H-E-B today has 240 stores in 125 Texas communities and 45,000 partners—as H-E-B refers to its employees. H-E-B is one of the nation's largest independently owned retail grocery chains. And

though the company competes on a price/value footing, service and community involvement are expressed and emphasize core values; values that are practiced, not just preached.

On the corporate side, H-E-B is a "5%" company, donating five percent of its pretax profit to charities each year. In addition, there is H-E-B Education 2000; a Food Bank Assistance Program, which gives 15 million pounds of food to nonprofit agencies; and at Christmas and Thanksgiving, H-E-B sponsors *Feasts of Sharing Dinners* in twenty communities across Texas and northern Mexico, serving over 120,000 meals.

The care and attention H-E-B partners pay customers is no less impressive than the corporate effort. Stories of employees who change flats, start uncooperative cars, and retrieve locked-in car keys are daily occurrences. It's just part of the H-E-B way. So is dropping off pharmacy prescriptions for ill patients, helping wheelchair bound customers in and out of their cars, and helping elderly customers home when their grocery burdens seem too much for their frail constitutions.

Then there are the things they do that seem, well, beyond simple explanation—and motivated by something far more fundamental than simply a concern for customer service or repeat business. Witness these three tales shared with us by Carol Olander, Vice President of Customer Service.

When ex-San Antonio resident Gloria Silvas wanted to honor her daughter's high school graduation with a special authentic Texas meal, her first call went out to H-E-B. So naturally, H-E-B partner Evelyn Gregorczyk, froze, wrapped, boxed, and shipped the fixings to Gloria—in California.

Michael Graze had been looking forward to his birthday party; he and his mom had planned it out in great detail, inviting many of his school chums. So when the six year old's Power Rangers birthday cake from the local H-E-B arrived with Michael spelled "M-I-C-H-E-L-E" he was distraught. The great centerpiece of the party had turned to an object of derision through a spelling error! He swore he could never show his face in school again.

When H-E-Ber Julie McCoy heard of Michael's plight from his mother, she didn't hesitate. Apologies and refunds, she knew, would be small solace for a little boy's crushed spirit. So she arranged for a new cake and a new party—at a local children's amusement park, with Michael as host and H-E-B as benefactor.

Ida Nava, a pharmacy technician at the Victoria, TX, store, noticed a woman and three children through the front window of her store. Their dress was shabby and their behavior less than purposeful. Later, when she noticed them still there, she went out and engaged the woman in conversation. As Ida had suspected, the little family was in dire straits; no money, nowhere to stay.

Ida went back into the store and started calling local shelters. All were filled, so she began calling nearby motels. When she found one that had rooms available, she went ahead and made a reservation for two nights for the family.

Ida then enlisted Sandra Gravel, another H-E-B employee. Sandy and Ida filled a bag with groceries, then loaded the woman and her children into Sandy's car. They drove them to the motel, paid for the room for two nights and helped the woman get her children settled in. Ask Ida why, and her answer is simple, "Because it was the right thing to do."

Make no mistake, H-E-B is as hard charging and profit-oriented as any company in America. The grocery store business is a low margin, highly competitive business. But from chairman to cashier trainee, there is an understanding that there is more on the mind of the company than dollars and cents. When CEO Charles Butt, grandson of the founder says, "Our partners are not just part of a company, they are part of a community," and reminds all hands that "giving something back" to the community is an important value, it is powerfully freeing... and wonderfully refreshing.

Lands' End: The Catalog Company with a Barnful of Goodwill

On the books, *Lands' End* is classified as a mail-order merchandiser. But in truth, four out of five sales it rings up come via an 800 number. Over 14 million times a year—someone calls Lands' End and in two rings or less is ear to ear with a salesperson, trained to know every detail of every piece of merchandise in every one of the company's twelve different catalog publications—for a total of 211 million catalogs mailed in 1996.

But beyond their technical skill and knowledge, Lands' End sales and service reps take pride in going above and beyond for customers with more complex needs than simply ordering the red polo shirt on page 11 or the denim skirt on page 5. We've heard incredible stories. A woman loses 40 pounds and decides to celebrate by ordering a new Lands' End wardrobe; a Specialty Shopper spends more than an hour on the phone with her coordinating all the choices. The mother of a blind seventeen-year-old who's planning to go off to college delegates to Lands' End the delicate task of picking out a wardrobe of slacks, shirts, sweaters, and jacket that can be worn in any combination—and without making him stand out in a crowd for all the wrong reasons. A young man moving from Dallas, TX, to Madison, WI to

attend college knew but two things about Wisconsin: winters are cold and Lands' End. He called the latter, asking for information on the former. The service rep who took the call spent 30 minutes on the phone giving a list of nice places to live—and good places to eat.

When we asked Beverly Holmes and Richard Mensch of Lands' End customer relations, if they could share some unique service stories with us, a 2-inch packet landed on our door step. Here's a sampling of the "above and beyond" service that goes out the door with the khaki pants and polo shirts and canvas brief cases 364 days of the year from Dodgeville, WI to Lands' End customers around the world, in the words of the four of the many customers who received it and two of the associates who provided it.

Dear Lands' End,

Recognizing that all good things must come to an end, I was still a little sad opening my very last Rugby Bear under the soft lights of my family Christmas tree. The bears had been a cherished annual gift from my family since my freshman year of college, so Kid Kodiak marked the end of an era for me.

I immediately fell in love with Kid's cute scowl, pot-belly, and affinity for blueberry pies. But something was missing—one little thing that kept me from being totally happy at getting the final member of my team.

That one little thing? Big Daddy, from 1992. I don't know how, but somehow the bear for that year did not make it under the tree. I realized it too late and it appeared impossible to get him. Lands' End phone reps said it was too late and he couldn't be ordered anymore. So I dropped it and tried to be content that I had the other six bears. But still...

Imagine my surprise when I opened up one of my last presents from my boyfriend and found—BIG DADDY! I was absolutely stunned—how could he have gotten this if LE said it was not available anymore?

I don't have the complete details from him yet (and maybe it's best that way to keep some of the "magic" of Christmas), but apparently he spoke with someone in Customer Service who helped him track down the "owner" of the `26 Championship team with the use of an internal newsletter for the employees of Lands' End.

So this is my little way of saying thanks to the mystery woman in Customer Service for helping beyond the call of duty, the mystery employee who contributed Big Daddy, and Lands' End for being the best company. This was truly one of the best Christmases ever!

And if I may, a huge public thank you for my boyfriend, Patrick. My Christmas present for him this year? A Lands' End travel golf bag, of course! (He loved it!)

Jennifer Jordan

Salisbury, NC

PS. Are you sure I can't convince you to conjure up a few more teammates???

Dear Lands' End,

I am writing to tell you how happy I am with your company. I ordered a tie for my husband for Christmas and it matched perfectly! The exciting part about this is that I and one of your patient customer service people matched the tie OVER-THE-PHONE to a shirt (not one of yours) my sister had bought him for his birthday.

The shirt was white with stripes of navy, burgundy, and tan. The burgundy had a brownish-rusty tint to it and the tan matched the particular tan shading of one of your shirts. So, armed with this information and understanding of my husband's conservative tastes, we found a tie (it "only" took 15 minutes) that matched the three colors in my shirt. The tie matches perfectly! I'm happy and so is my sister, since my husband had no other tie to wear with this shirt!

Thank you Lands' End for your "wonderfulness."

Sincerely,

Annemarie Ciskanik

Dear Lands' End,

Recently something funny happened that I thought I'd share with you. In my apartment building, there are some people who have a store on the first floor which sells children's clothing. One day I was walking into the building with my order that I had just received from Lands' End. The owner of the store, Mr. Watanabe, stopped me and said "Lands' End?" Mr. Watanabe doesn't speak English, so this was a big sentence for him. I said yes, and because I was halfway up the stairs, I told him that I'd come back with the catalog. Later I helped him make out his order and send it properly. He was really happy.

A few weeks later, he called me into the shop. He had gotten the order from Lands' End, but one of the items didn't come. There was a letter with the part that came. He could figure most of it out, but halfway down, there was a phrase that gave him a problem. It said, "Bear with us, we're doing the best we can."

He asked me, "Bear with us, what's that?" He told me in Japanese what he thought it meant. "Kuma to isshon ni irun desu." Translated back to English it means, "there is a bear here with us."

"The order is slow because there is a bear in the factory?" he asked. I almost died laughing.

I straightened him out, and the shirt eventually did come, but every time I think about things being backordered now, I wonder if there's a bear in your factory.

Yours truly,

Mark Oesterlin
Handa City, Japan

From: Ruth Shober

To: LE Product Room Peak Staff

Subject: Stain Removal

The following experiment was prompted by a call that I had last week. Seems a customer dropped her dark colored ketch purse in the street, thereby staining it with road salt. She wanted to know what to do to get the stain out. I was concerned that the road salt might have some sort of bleaching agent in it. My husband said it is merely sodium chloride, and has very minute amounts of a coloring agent to make it blue. It also has anticaking agents.

So...I went down to Highway 12 and scooped up some slush with salt in it and brought it home. I put some dark burgundy fabric, very similar to the sailcloth in the ketch purse, into the slush and let it dry overnight. Sure enough, there was a big ugly stain on the fabric. I took a metal bristle brush and got rid of the excess salt, then got the fabric slightly damp and brushed it again. "Voila," the stain was gone.

(Now you know how I get my kicks when I'm not working at LE!)

Ruth

Within the mound of stories we received from Beverly at Lands' End were several tales told over the company e-mail system lauding the work of fellow employees. One caught our eye for several reasons. It was a note from Nancy Gavin, a customer sales lead person, lauding the work of three colleagues in three different physical locations who worked together to create an ensemble for a blind customer, who had written back praising the work of the trio. Above Nancy's signature was a salutation that says more than anything we could ever pen about the spirit and determination of the people who make it happen at Lands' End.

> "Nothing is impossible to a willing heart."

Cadillac's Roadside Service Serves Up Great Saves for Customers

Corporations are constantly in search of ways to distinguish themselves in their customers' eyes. General Motors Cadillac division came up with a great one when it invented Cadillac Roadside Service. The program, begun in 1988, promises Cadillac owners:

> "Cadillac's extraordinary Roadside Service is more than an auto club or towing service. More than 1,800 Cadillac factory trained dealer technicians, with over 600 GM Suburbans, participate in this on-call service. Cadillac Roadside Service can be reached by dialing 1-800-882-1112, 24 hours a day, 365 days a year. A Cadillac trained advisor will assist you, and in many cases the problem can be resolved over the phone. If it becomes necessary, Cadillac's integrated communications system will transfer all essential information to the nearest trained dealer technician in seconds, and dispatch the technician to your location. Armed with tools, parts, key making equipment and cellular phones, the technician can handle most roadside repairs. Cadillac Roadside Service can also assist with jump-starts, towing, lock outs, flat tire changes and fuel deliveries. These services are provided at no charge for any warranty-covered situation, and at a nominal charge if your Cadillac is no longer under warranty."

From its inception, Cadillac's Roadside Service has garnered raves from customers. Apart from the expected jump-starts, fan belt replacements, tire changing, and tows, the Roadside technicians have prided themselves on exceeding customer expectations, adding style, flair, and a unique personal touch to their service.

Technically, Doug Paulson was on vacation. He was already 425 miles south of his Chicago-area home, passing by the Peru, IL, exits on the freeway, when he spotted a 1992 DeVille off the shoulder and across the median. At the next exit Paulson reversed course and came to the aid of owner Gary Braud, who had run out of gas. And of course, there was no charge for the rescue or the gas. "I hadn't even called anyone!" reported an astonished Braud.

Joan Seidel's problem wasn't major. A battery cable had come loose and her car wouldn't start. But standing there in the grocery store parking lot in Pittsburgh, PA, it seemed a major catastrophe was unfolding. And when Roadside technician Bob Lutz arrived it was obvious to him that Ms. Seidel was a bit shaken. So after he tightened the connector and started the car, he followed her home, helped her into her house and, of course, helped her put away the groceries.

Though the service is in its tenth year, Cadillac owners continue to be astonished by the thoroughness and responsiveness of the Roadside technicians. And the letters pour in.

An impressed customer, in California, was moved to write:

My husband has Alzheimer's disease, and boy do I need Roadside Service. My husband cannot drive, so I have to. When I used your service a few weeks ago, I was so overwhelmed. The gentleman I spoke with was so kind, patient, and courteous. I asked the man where he was coming from and he told me. I told him 30 miles was too far away and 9:30 at night was too late to come. The gentleman said, "Mrs. Amantea, I'm leaving now to help you. It's my job. Please don't worry about the distance I'm traveling."

As the only driver, I appreciate Roadside Service. It relieves a lot of my worries. For me it's the best service you can offer. That night when I needed help, all of your employees were outstanding.

Alice Amantea
Orangeville, CA

Sometimes the services rendered by Cadillac's "rescue rangers of the open road" is as memorable to them as it is to the customers they serve. Witness Anthony Harris of Richmond, CA's recent brush with fame:

As a Cadillac Roadside Service technician, Anthony "Heavy T" Harris thought that his nickname was the closest brush with fame he would ever have.

Friends had given him the nickname because of his resemblance to rap music artist "Heavy D"—at least before Harris lost 86 pounds last year.

But early one morning in March, Heavy T got a call from the set of the *Nash Bridges* television show. The coordinators of the show, which stars Don Johnson, were frantic because a 1994

Cadillac Seville they planned to use in a stunt refused to start. Luckily they stumbled across a Roadside Service card in the glove box and made a call for help. Heavy T sprang out of bed and into action.

He raced to the set in San Francisco and began to examine the Seville. But everything checked out fine—that is, until someone tried to fill the car's fuel tank.

"While I was looking at the car, some guy tried to fill up the gas tank," Heavy T explains. "But it was full, so fuel spilled all over the ground."

Keen instincts and a funny smell coming from the spilled fuel told Heavy T what he needed to know. The car had been filled with diesel fuel, not gasoline.

Knowing that the gas tank and fuel pump would have to be removed, Heavy T called George Cincery of McNevin Cadillac— who was at home—to help with instructions for some of the more complex parts of the repair. The entire overhaul was completed in less than 3 hours.

"The car smoked a lot, but it ran," says Heavy T. "They did the stunt, and, at the end, they blew up the car. It was great."

The producers thought it was great, too, and gave Heavy T an autographed *Nash Bridges* t-shirt for saving the day.

Stories and background contributed by
Mary Ann Jeffery and H. Scott Bicknell

American Express: Encouraging and Celebrating Great Performances

On January 17, 1995 an earthquake devastated the Osaka/Kobe area of south central Japan. Eight members of the Osaka office of American Express—an office destroyed in the quake—immediately set up shop in temporary quarters in Osaka and Tokyo, and worked a grueling day and night schedule of providing emergency service to customers. They arranged evacuations, emergency replacements for lost travel documents, passports and visas, and made emergency cash advances. All this despite the fact that every member of the team had suffered a loss of personal property or damage to a home and for some, even personal injury.

Does the Osaka team's dedication to serving American Express customers seem extreme? In some companies perhaps, but at Amex it is just one story in a rich history of exceptional customer service. Each year since 1982, this tradition of exceptional service has been officially celebrated through a worldwide company recognition program called Great Performers. The program recognizes employees "who deliver outstanding service

above and beyond their job responsibilities to external customers, and who exemplify the value of placing the interests of
clients and customers first."

Each year several hundred Amex employees are nominated
for their efforts in each of the company's eight worldwide re-
gions. Regional winners become eligible for the company-wide
recognition program, and a trip to New York City for the Grand
Award Winners recognition dinner. Thirty-five super service
stories were recognized in 1995 and the associates connected
with them so honored.

In addition to the Osaka/Kobe team, other honorees were:

Laurie DeLaRosa, of Troy, MI, who came to the aid of a customer
and his family, traveling from Paris, France to Detroit for surgery
on their baby. She made air reservations, arranged ground transportation, booked a hotel suite, and then went to the airport on her
day off to assist the nervous mother with child care as they waited
for the husband to arrive and rendezvous for the trip to the
hospital.

Barbara Renaud and Donna Katona of Ontario, Canada, helped a
cardholder whose son and daughter-in-law had been unknow-
ingly exposed to a deadly strain of meningitis, locate the couple
and see that they were administered a lifesaving vaccine. The customer was in Ontario, the couple in Venezuela. Amexers in Cara-
cas put an alert out to all Venezuelan establishments that accept
the American Express charge card. The couple was found in 24
hours.

Nancy Boccardo of Langhorn, PA, received a call from a customer
whose car broke down en route to the airport—with a client in
tow. Boccardo left her office, picked up the customer and his
client, drove them the remaining 40 miles in time to catch the
client's flight. She then arranged to have the customer's car taken
to a garage for repairs and drove him back to his office.

Abraham Punnoose and Chetan Goswamy of the Bombay, India,
office received a call from a customer who had lost all of his travel

documents, cash and credit cards and for the last 30 hours had been held incommunicado in immigration at the Bombay airport. Punnoose convinced the counsel general in New Delhi to go to the airport and issue a replacement passport. In the meantime, Goswamy made new travel arrangements for the customer and personally delivered emergency funds and new airline tickets to him at the airport.

What *else* did the Amex Great Performers do in the name of customer service? Patricia Miller of Greensboro, NC, foiled an attempted kidnapping. Pedro De Regil of Cancun, Mexico, came to the rescue of two customers who had been mistakenly detained by Mexican police as suspects in an armed robbery. Maree Mantanle of Sydney, Australia, arranged for a cardholder's son, taken ill while traveling in Africa, to be transferred to a hospital where care was available for his condition. And Nisreen Nauguib of Cairo, Egypt? All *she* did was arrange for the daughter of a frantic customer to be transported from Egypt to Italy for lifesaving, emergency surgery on a spinal tumor in a matter of hours—circumventing the weeks of international travel paperwork that might've cost the girl's life.

Why do the Amex account reps and travel advisors and credit advisors put themselves out like this? For the trip to New York for the dinner with senior management and a certificate to hang on the office wall? More likely, it is because that's the way things are done and expected to be done at the company. In the words of Amex chairman Harvey Golub speaking at the 1995 dinner and ceremony, "Their deeds help create an emotional tie that inspires customer loyalty and serves as a model for us all."

Contributed by Gail Wasserman

Federal Express: Where Customers Absolutely, Positively Come First

Since its inception in 1973, Federal Express has thrived on providing exceptional service to its customers. The company's core service—guaranteed overnight delivery of documents and small parcels to virtually any place on the face of the earth—set a new standard in the courier business. Today the company delivers 2.8 million items each day to destinations in the United States and 212 countries including such out-of-the-way destinations as Bhutan, Palau, and Surinam, and has recently entered the same-day delivery business in the United States.

In addition to the on-demand package delivery business, Federal Express manages the global distribution of Laura Ashley fashion products and the operation of a distribution network in Singapore for national Semiconductor Corp. Producing the Federal Express magic requires a fleet of nearly 600 airplanes, 38,000 delivery vehicles, over 130,000 employees, and millions of dollars of sophisticated technology.

But technology isn't the real story behind Federal Express. It's people. In fact, the company's motto is: "People, Service and Profits"—and the order of priorities is no accident. From its very earliest days, Federal Express has placed a premium on hiring, training, and retaining good people and turning them lose with a mandate to make Federal Express customers feel well served.

What follows are a smattering of Federal Express Bravo Zulu, Golden Falcon, and Humanitarian Award service stories as they were reported through the *FedEx World Update*, the company's internal newspaper.

A college professor in Spartenburg, SC, had called FedEx for a pickup at his home, then left to run a quick errand. Upon returning, he was surprised to find FedEx courier Bruce's van at the curb. Let the professor tell it, as he did in his letter to the company.

> Soon after I pulled into my driveway, a man, who evidently had just broken into my home, bolted out my front door. I ran to the truck, and the courier, realizing immediately what was happening, told me to call 911 while he chased the runaway suspect. Bruce chased him indeed and consequently was able to provide the police not only with an outstanding description of the suspect, but also having followed the suspect to a waiting car, recorded information that could well lead to the suspect's apprehension. Bruce acted coolly and quickly. I cannot thank him enough for his willingness to become involved and for his very real help. Federal Express is an outstanding business. It also clearly employs outstanding people.

When Juneau, Alaska courier Mark arrived for a pickup, he noticed that the elderly woman seemed confused. She explained that a man had called from New York City to say she had won a cash prize of $100,000. To get it, however, she must send a "tax" payment of $3,500 right away to a Canadian address. The seventy-seven-year-old customer had gone to the bank for a cashier's check, then called FedEx.

Red flags went up for Mark. He earnestly talked the lady out of sending the money. "He seemed so sure of himself," she said. The courier advised the woman to call the police and the state attorney general's office, and to make sure he called the police himself. "She was a real sweetheart," Mark said.

Alice is a senior service agent at FedEx. Late on a Friday morning, she learned from one of the FedEx customer inquiry centers that an overnight shipment of medicine bound for a customer in her area had gone astray. The customer, she finds out, had brain cancer and had taken the last dose in her possession—and the time for her next dose was looming.

Despite her efforts, Alice was unable to locate the errant shipment. To compound matters, Alice had also come to realize that the customer had neither transportation—nor the funds—to travel to a pharmacy for an emergency supply of the medication, enough to tide her over until Monday, when a fresh replacement shipment would arrive from the distant medical center.

Alice resolved the dilemma by driving to the pharmacy herself, picking up and paying for the prescription, and delivering it to the customer in person. And when the customer asked how she could thank her, Alice asked that she send a letter of thanks to the pharmacist who had filled the prescription and entrusted it to her for delivery.

Las Vegas courier Kirk was making a residential delivery nearby when he spotted a police officer pursuing a pipe-wielding suspect on an elementary school ground. The officer drew his pistol, subduing the suspect. When he holstered his weapon, however, the suspect knocked him to the ground. The officer resumed his pursuit and was knocked to the ground again. That's when Kirk, a bodybuilder of impressive size, stepped in with, "It's over, dude." He held the attacker until the officer could complete his arrest. Observed from classrooms, Kirk was a hero to the students. They asked him to speak to a class. He agreed and chose community responsibility and good citizenship as his topic. The students gave him a poster: "Kirk is our hero—we love FedEx." The courier himself kept quiet about the episode, it was reported by another customer who then called the FedEx 800 number. "Kirk truly displays a commitment to Federal Express and the community in which we serve," said his operations manager when recommending him for the Humanitarian Award.

A few years ago one of us was on a conference panel with a Federal Express senior operations executive. A questioner from the audience asked if it were true that Federal Express employees were expected to do whatever it took to serve their customers. "Yes," the executive replied, "they certainly are." The questioner pressed on, relating a story he'd seen in a local paper recounting a part a FedEx employee had played in a dramatic rescue of a child, and how the employee had commandeered a standby Federal Express jet to bring a critical piece of equipment to the site of the rescue. "Yes, I saw that same story," the exec replied, "no doubt it happened."

"But, but, "stammered the questioner, "how do you go about authorizing such extraordinary things in the middle of the night?"

"You're asking whether I or some other senior manager personally authorized the use of company equipment for this purpose, aren't you?" answered the Fed Ex manager.

"Yes, I certainly am," demanded the questioner.

The executive from FedEx smiled and gave the finest explanation of empowering people to serve their customers we've ever heard. "If that employee had even thought about calling someone to ask permission in that situation, I would have been disappointed. No one in our company would have ever denied such a request—and it's my job to be sure he understands that—going in. Sir, sooner or later you have to trust your people to do the right thing at the right time. And I do."

8

Tales From the Service Zone

We know, as do you, that it's important to speak and think well of your customers. Nothing turns away customers faster than an obvious disdain and lack of respect. And customers know in their bones when the people they're dealing with have an attitude or think they're somehow "better" than their customers—or that their customers are somehow strange or their concerns laughable.

That said, it is also true that customers can inadvertently—and sometimes with tongue planted firmly in cheek—say and do odd, interesting and very, very funny things. Remembering, recounting, sharing, and enjoying such incidents doesn't show disrespect—just a fine sense of fun and appreciation for the accidental, the serendipitous, the misspoken, and the willfully witty.

Since beginning the "Knock Your Socks Off Service" series, we have invited customer service people we've met around the world to share stories of customer service situations with us—and they have. As we noted in the beginning, most of the stories in this book have come from them—or rather, from you—the customer service pros who day-after-day make their customers happy campers. In addition to the stories of heroism and service above and beyond, you and they have often shared with us the memorable and the strange, the unusual and the funny, the perplexing and the zany that add spice and, yes, a laugh or two to life on the firing line.

Presented on the following pages, then, is a compendium of reports from The Service Zone—a small side trip to a land where Rod Serling would feel right at home. We offer here for your casual entertainment and enjoyment some of the most unusual, amusing, and pithy things customers and customer service employees report hearing and seeing—and sometimes saying themselves. May they brighten your day just a little bit, and serve to remind you why you get up in the morning, brush your teeth, comb your hair, rush off to the office or store, take that first phone call, look that first customer in the eye, put a smile in your voice and ask, "Good Morning. How may I help you?"

Oddities From the Edge

From 1988 to 1996, Lakewood Publications' *Service Edge Newsletter* chronicled the growing, worldwide, service economy, and the attention corporations and organization's afforded customer care. And from time to time, we stopped to examine the lighter side of customer relations as well. So, from The Outer Edge of the Service Zone, come these tales.

According to *USA Today*, a customer of Old National Bank in Spokane, WA, walked in the bank to cash a $100 check. He also asked a receptionist if he could have his parking slip validated, to save 60 cents. The receptionist refused, saying the customer hadn't conducted a "valid" transaction; she told him he had to make a deposit to qualify for the parking credit.

"I told her I'm considered a substantial depositor, and she looked at me like...well," said John Barrier, 59, the customer, who was wearing dirty construction clothes at the time. Barrier then asked to see the bank manager, who also refused to stamp the ticket.

Barrier then contacted bank headquarters, vowing to withdraw his money—$ 2 million plus—unless the manager apologized. No call came. "So the next day I went over and the first amount I took out was $1 million," Barrier says. "If you have $100 in a bank or $1 million, I think they owe you the courtesy of stamping your parking ticket." When no apology was forthcoming, Mr. Barrier went back and withdrew a second million dollars. And by that evening, says Barrier, he received a great deal of attention from the bank. And his 60 cents back.

The Mall of America, the gargantuan shopping/entertainment complex in Bloomington, MN, invests heavily in its top-notch, multilingual customer service staff. On an average day, service reps hand out some 50,000 directories and maps. In an average week, they dole out 15,000 strollers, 14,000 wheelchairs, and 5,000 carts.

As trained professionals, they are skilled at handling all requests with a smile. Or almost all, it seems.

The *Minneapolis Star Tribune* reports that a woman approached one of the mall customer service desks and handed a small cooler to a service rep. She asked the smiling young man if he would watch her, uh, urine samples while she shopped. Momentarily flustered, he quickly recovered and called the mall's Group Health office for an assist.

On another occasion, a customer brought in a box and asked the reps to watch her snake eggs while she shopped. She said they were about to hatch and had to be fed immediately upon hatching. Could a staff employee, perhaps, page her when the blessed event occurred? Without pausing to ask about the species of the snake or consider the service ramifications, a Mall service rep firmly, but politely requested that the woman take the eggs back to her car.

Producer Bob Bastanchurly of television station KLAL-TV in Los Angeles, CA, received a call from an irate viewer. "How can you possibly consider a program called *The Great Chefs of Rwanda*? With all the death and destruction, disease and famine in that country, how could you be so crass?" she demanded.

After he calmed the caller, Bastanchurly reassured her that she had simply misheard the promotional spot in question, "We were advertising an interview with the producer of the show *Great Chefs* which was to air on another syndicated talk show, *Rolanda!*"

Michael Sullivan of Reprint Book Shop in Washington, DC, was manning the cash register during the noontime rush, when a woman elbowed her way to the front of the line, demanding his attention—and help—in finding a book she'd been sent to purchase. The line at the register lengthened as she dug into her huge purse, looking for the slip of paper she'd written the title on. Finally withdrawing a well worn piece of notebook paper from the depths, she announced, "Here it is!" and handed it to Sullivan. Relieved that this mini-ordeal was about to end, he unfolded the paper, upon which were written the words, "Number one bestseller from Coast to Coast."

Customer research at Greyhound Lines of Canada showed that dirty bathrooms were making a bad impression on customers. So John Munro, Greyhound's senior vice president for marketing and operations, sent a message to employees about the need to manage "the little things." He also started making regular surprise visits to Greyhound's 570 terminals and dining with the local manager—*in the bathroom.*

"I wanted to get a feel for what the company looked like from the customer's point of view," Munro says. "About half my managers thought I was totally crazy, and the other half thought I was totally committed to customer service."

Munro gives top marks to the women's restroom in the Vancouver, British Columbia, Canada, terminal, where he ate duck and drank champagne with a regional manager.

The Zone Archives

The *Reader's Digest* is a wonderful archive of Service Zone antics. Over the magazine's 75 years, the editors have faithfully chronicled the endless variety of ways that serving customers can surprise and delight server and served alike. The following four are among our favorites.

"Bonanza, Good morning," my brother Glenn said when he picked up the phone at his car dealership, Bonanza Corvettes. The caller asked about their hours, and my bother explained that they opened at nine, but closed between noon and 1 P.M.

"You mean you're closed between twelve and one?" the caller asked.

"Yes. That's when we go to lunch," Glen replied.

"You must be joking!" the man said.

"Hey, we've got to eat," Glenn said.

"That's the most ridiculous thing I've ever heard!" the caller declared. The conversation grew even more tense until they realized that the caller had the wrong number. He had been trying to reach the Bonanza Steak House.

Contributed by Susan Haight

I took my daughter, who was twelve years old, for a medical checkup. After waiting for 2 hours, we finally made it to the examining room, but waited another 30 minutes for the doctor to appear.

While examining my daughter, the doctor asked if she had shown any signs of going through puberty. "Yes," I replied. "She went through it while we were in your waiting room."

Contributed by Carole J. Hart

A customer called our airline's reservation office to pay for his ticket with a credit card. My co-worker asked him, "Would you please spell the name as it appears on the card, sir?"

The customer replied, "V-I-S-A."

Contributed by Cathy Mosely

One Saturday I rushed to the supermarket to get groceries for a big Sunday dinner. At home, however, I noticed the checker had charged me $1.68 for the ham instead of $16.80. My husband quickly drove to the store with the ham and the receipt, but the checker said it was her mistake and that there would be no extra charge. Pleased with his honest efforts, my husband then return to his car—only to find a $15 parking ticket attached to the windshield!

Contributed by Carol Taler

Customers Say the Darnedest Things

We have conducted several contests in which we asked customer service people to share the strange and delightful things their customers have offered up in the heat of contact. And share they have! We've received thousands of snippets from service pros in a dozen industries from high tech to building maintenance. What follows are a reprise of some of our favorites.

Overcome by Technology—Hi and Low

Computers take the measure of everyone from time to time. Sometimes it's something as seemingly simple as finding the on/off switch that sends the new computer user running for the customer service helpline.

Sometimes it's simply the need to register their frustrations that sends users to the phones.

Customer:	"I've pushed and pushed on the foot pedal and I can't get this computer started."
CSR:	"Foot pedal?"
Customer:	"Yea, this white thing with the little ball on the bottom and the clicker at the top."

Anonymous

Library Patron:	"Do you have computers here?"
Librarian:	"Yes."
Patron:	"And you keep a record of the books on it?"
Librarian:	"Yes."
Patron:	"Oh good. Could you ask it which books I've read? I forget and I don't want to read any of `em over again."

Contributed by Terrie Miller
Anoka Co. Library
Anoka, MN

CSR:	"You'll have to make up a new password."
Customer:	"Okay."
(Long pause)	
CSR:	"Sir? What's happening?"
Customer:	"I made up a new password and nothing happened. OH! Was I supposed to key it in?"

Contributed by Rich Simek
Grumman Data Systems
Long Island, NY

Computers aren't the only source of confusion in our lives. Lesser technological wonders lay bare our foibles from time to time as well.

- "Could you please tell me which speed dial button you are on my telephone?"

Contributed by Sherri Holdeman
First of America Services
Kalamazoo, MI

- "This car battery charger—can I just plug it into my car cigarette lighter then connect it to my battery to recharge it?"

Contributed by A.L. Thrasher
Thrasher's Hardware
Des Moines, IA

CSR:	"We can fax those papers if you'd like."
Customer:	"Oh, we don't have a fax. But we do have a Xerox machine—will that work?"

Contributed by Colleen Bonneville
Norwest Funding
Minneapolis, MN

Is There a Doctor in the House—Or Somebody?

Navigating the modern healthcare delivery system and the web of insurance providers that pay for it can confuse even the most sophisticated among us.

Caller:	"I had a whole bunch of tests done yesterday by my doctor."
Insurance CSR:	"Yes?"
Caller:	"I called my doctor but he's not in."
Insurance CSR:	"Yes?"
Caller:	"Well, can't *you* tell me what's wrong with me?"

Contributed by Mike Kata
CIGNA Healthcare
Bristol, CT

- "Isn't `neurology' and `urology' the same except for the spelling?"

Contributed by Ava Parker

- "A tree in my yard fell on my head. Is my medical treatment covered under my homeowner's policy?"

Contributed by Sarane Heggen
PriPac
Hinsdale, IL

Dollars and Nonsense

Maybe it's the arithmetic. Certainly it's all the "gee-whiz" stories about the marriage of high tech and financial management, and what the really smart investor should be doing today that raise our expectations—and confusion level. Whatever the origin, we are indeed muddled by matters financial.

Customer: "Why did you bounce my check? It says void if written for less than $100. I wrote if for more than that!"

CSR: "How much did you write it for?"

Customer: "$19,000."

CSR: "I'm sorry, but you only have $2,000 in your account."

Customer: "I guess I'll have to take the car back."

Contributed by Kirstin Tompkins
Oppenheimer Funds
Denver, CO

Customer: "You keep sending me these notices about being overdrawn on my account."

CSR: "Yes sir, that's correct."

Customer: "But I have one of those special revolving accounts."

CSR: "Sir?"

Customer: "Yea. I write checks all month, then at the end, you tell me what I owe, right?"

Contributed by Carol Peloso
The Citizens Banking Co.
Alliance, OH

Service Encounters of an Even Stranger Kind

There are days when every other customer seems to have slept under the bed *and* gotten up on the wrong side as well. And then there are those days when every third customer is truly on vacation from the Twilight Zone. By quitting time you feel just a little bit like calling out, "Beam me up, Scotty. I've been here way too long!"

Customer:	"I'm calling to follow-up on a complaint letter I wrote about one of your motel managers.
CSR:	"Yes sir, I have it here."
Customer:	"I was never informed of the `no pets' policy when I made the reservation. Then I was asked to leave. Outrageous!"
CSR:	"If you didn't know there was a no pet policy, why were you pushing your dog through the bathroom window when the manager walked in?"

Contributed by Lori Nehlich
Super 8 Motels
Aberdeen, SD

Customer: "After I pick up my rental car in Honolulu, can I drive from island to island?"

Contributed by Leisure Travel
Los Angeles, CA

Caller: "I want to start a subscription."
CSR: "Great, what's your address?"
Caller: "I'm not sure, I just live here in the winters."
CSR: "I'm afraid I need an address."
Caller: "Come on. I'm in Apache Junction right across from the Circle K store. You know where that is."

Contributed by Iris Oligschlaeger
Phoenix Newspapers Inc.
Phoenix, AZ

Customer:	"Is this the cable company?"
CSR:	"Yes, sir."
Customer:	"You need to fix my converter box."
CSR:	"What seems to be the problem."
Customer:	"Every night about 3:00 A.M. it starts playing wine cooler theme songs."

Contributed by David Levenson
New Channels Corp.
East Syracuse, NY

Newspapers seem to receive a disproportionate number of calls from denizens of `The Zone' who are in search of perfect service.

- "Can you have my carrier get down and ring my door bell when she delivers my paper? My alarm clock doesn't work so well."

Contributed by Jesse Luna
Arizona Republic Newspapers
Phoenix, AZ

When *Frankfort Times* customer service specialist Brenda Beaven's photo appeared in the paper, along with the note that she stood ready to help customers, a subscriber called and asked what days Brenda had available, explaining.

"I can get in and out of bed, but could use assistance with a few things around the house."

Contributed by Tammy Janz
The Frankfort Times
Frankfort, IN

Thank You for Sharing That...I Think

Every customer service person has had the urge to blurt out, "Please don't tell me any more. I already know more than I want to." That impulse is often followed closely by the dreaded urge to add "I know I'm going to regret this, but why do you ask?"

- "So let's say that I went hunting in the mountains and say I rented a mule, and say there was an accident, and say the mule was accidentally shot. Would you pay for the mule under my homeowners policy?"

  Contributed by Connie Willcox
  National General Insurance Co.
  St. Louis, MO

- "About this application. I'm in the middle of a sex change operation. So which name do I put on the account, his or hers?"

  Contributed by Debbie Pierce
  Central Illinois Lighting Co.
  Peoria, IL

- "If I fertilize my lawn this morning, will I be able to go shopping this afternoon?"

  Contributed by Dru Gibson
  The Scotts Co.
  Marysville, OH

Oh, Never Mind

Sometimes customers, and customer service people alike, are sure that they are absolutely positively right—until the dawn comes. Then, well. "Never mind."

- "Hello. I just called in and spoke with Dave. And I told him the roses and lilacs I bought from you were dead and I wasn't going to pay for them. Well, when I got off the phone my husband told me they were just planted on the other side of the house, and I hadn't seen them yet. So, never mind."

Contributed by Wendy Braun
Foster & Galagher, Inc.
Peoria, IL

Customer:	"Do you remember when I called and told you that the meter reader stole the chicken that was defrosting on my counter?"
CSR:	"Yes."
Customer:	"And you remember that you sent a supervisor out to find the meter reader and get my chicken back?"
CSR:	"Yes."
Customer:	"Well, my husband didn't want chicken for dinner, and he put it back in the freezer. So, never mind."

Contributed by Ann Purvee
Rochester Gas & Electric
Rochester, NY

Subscriber: "Is this the paper?"
CSR: "Yes, may I help you?"
Subscriber: "I want to know what you're going to do about refunds?"
CSR: "Refunds?"
Subscriber: "You bet. The front page of your paper says `Final Edition' and I'm paid up for the last of the month."

Contributed by Jim Batt
Phoenix Newspapers, Inc.
Phoenix, AZ

Patron: "How dare you charge full price for these books. They're all used. I can buy brand new ones any place in town."
Librarian: "But ma'am, we don't sell them, we loan them out. Free."
Patron: "Oh. Never mind."

Contributed by Kathy B.
Anoka County Library
Anoka, MN

Finally, there are some things customers say that are eternal, universal, and transcendent. They give us solace that, amidst all the change around us, some things endure forever. This reported by Ann Wilson, Central Illinois Lighting Company, Peoria, IL, makes the point with gold stars.

> Customer: "My dog ate my disconnect notice."
> Ms. Wilson: "Is there any reason why you didn't call us when your dog ate the notice?"
> Customer: "He ate the phonebook, too!"

About the Authors

Ron Zemke is a management consultant and researcher who has become one of the best-known and most widely quoted authorities on the continuing service revolution. As senior editor of *TRAINING* magazine and a syndicated columnist, he has covered the emergence and development of the global service economy. Ron has authored or co-authored twenty-three books including the best-selling *Knock Your Socks Off Service* series. In 1994, he was awarded the MOBIUS award by the Society of Consumer Affairs Professionals and in 1995 he was named one of the "New Quality Gurus" by *Quality Digest* magazine.

Kristin Anderson is an internationally recognized customer service workshop leader and keynote speaker. She also has extensive experience in focus group and survey research. Her writing has appeared in numerous publications including *HR Magazine*, *Boardroom Reports*, *Computing Channels* and *Mobius*. Kristin has co-authored four of the volumes in the *Knock Your Socks Off Service* series and acts as host on six films on the customer service process. She is also author of *Great Customer Service on the Telephone* (AMACOM).

Performance Research Associates is one of North America's premier customer service/customer relations/service quality consulting firms. PRA has offices in Minneapolis, MN; Dallas, TX; and Ann Arbor, MI; providing training and consulting services to clients in North America, Europe, South America, and the Pacific rim. The *Knock Your Socks Off Service* series draws on the experience and work of the partners of Performance Research Associates, Inc. Readers interested in information about presentations, consulting, or other PRA services may contact the firm's Minneapolis office at 800/359-2576 or visit http://www.socksoff.com.

Contributors

Contributors 191

"Princely" Vendor Bails Out Victoria's Secret
Mark Ballard, Victoria's Secret, Columbus, OH

Not to Fear, the Contact Lens Express Is Here
Sharon Forshee Haukohl, Shop 'n Chek, Atlanta, GA

Trains, Planes, and Automobiles Make This Party Happen
Fiona Luhrs, Tranz Rail Limited, New Zealand

Chapter 3: Savoring Those "Daily Delights"

Kid's Meal for the Big Guy
Tami Cline, American School Food Service Association, Alexandria, VA

Salting Away a Snowbound Customer's Pain
JoAnn Mueller, Ace Hardware Corporation, Oak Brook, IL

"Good Samaritan" Travel Agency Eases Pain of Passenger with Dying Mother
Robyn Zimmermann, Professional Travel Corporation, Denver, CO

For the Colorado Rockies, Service Is Part of Their Game
Nicole Jacobsen, Colorado Rockies, Denver, CO

GE Answer Center Cooks Up a Big One
Merrell Grant, GE Answer Center, Louisville, KY

These Delivery Men Cometh—and Serve Up Delight
Ken Barry, Merchants Home Delivery Service, Oxnard, CA

Pampered Limo Passengers Avoid Being Smothered by Samsonite
John Bailey, Bailey Travel, York, PA

"People Over Paperwork" Philosophy Is Its Own Reward
Carol Haiar, Northwestern Mutual Life Insurance Company, Milwaukee, WI

St. Luke's Medical Center's Fan Mail Says It All
Allen Stasiewski, St. Luke's Medical Center, Milwaukee, WI

Small Kindnesses Enrich Both Giver and Receiver
Mary Wieth, Sheraton Hotel and Towers, Seattle, WA

Giving a Young Bone Marrow Patient a Crucial Lifeline to the Outside World
Patricia Southard, Oregon Health Sciences University, Portland, OR

Andersonville or Bust
John Quinley, National Park Service, Washington, DC

Chapter 4: Service from the Heart

Full Fare Service at a Discount Store
Pat Daniels, Target Stores, Minneapolis, MN

Nursing Homes with Heart
Beth Adair, Beverly Enterprises, Fort Smith, AR

Going to Bat for the Bereaved
Thomas J. Brueck, Bill Communications, LeSueur, MN
Sue Showers, Hamilton County Educational Service Center, Cincinnati, OH

The Great Floods of '97
Pioneer Planet
Grand Forks Herald
Minneapolis Star Tribune

An Angel's Kiss?
Patricia Southard, Oregon Health Service University, Portland, OR

Passing the Hat for a Troubled Customer
Cheri M. Garton, The Denver Water Company, Denver Water Company, Denver, CO

Remembering the Rescue Dogs of Oklahoma City
Kathy Davis, Hill's Pet Nutrition, Topeka, KS

Chapter 5: At Risk of Life and Limb

Insurance Reps Create Unique Road Rescue
Teresa Novacek and Victoria Cherne, Blue Cross Blue Shield of Minnesota, Minneapolis, MN

No Ordinary Public Utility Guys, These!
Mitch Basefsky, City of Tucson Water Department, Tucson, AZ
Lisa Parks, United Water of Florida, Jacksonville, Jacksonville, FL

Into Harm's Way: Two Tales of Hurricane Heroics
Matt Childs, Mitchell's Formal Wear, Raleigh, NC

UPS Highway Heroes Save Lives
Kristen Petrella, United Parcel Service, Atlanta, GA

Little Things Sometimes Mean More Than a Lot
Cathy Petit, Southwest Airlines, Dallas, TX

The $800 Thank-You Letter
Robert Franklin, *Minneapolis Star Tribune*, Minneapolis, MN

Breathing Life Into a Dying Dream
Dick Landis, Travel Agency Management Services, Minneapolis, MN

National Park Service Rangers to the Rescue
John Quinley, National Park Service, Washington, DC

Chapter 6: Memorable People

Patti Schutta: Always Time for That Little Extra Service
Karen Miller, Minnegasco, Minneapolis MN

Chapter 7: Keeping Great Company

Norwest Bank: Where Customers Are at the Heart of Service
Jill Packey, Norwest Corporation, Minneapolis, MN

H.E. Butt Grocery Stores: Where Great Service Is in the Bag
Carol Olander, H.E. Butt Grocery Company, San Antonio, TX

Lands' End: The Catalog Company with a Barnful of Goodwill
Beverly Holmes and Richard Mensch, Lands' End Company, Dodgeville, WI

Cadillac's Roadside Service Serves Up Great Saves for Customers
Mary Ann Jeffery and H. Scott Bicknell, Cadillac Motors, Warren, MI

American Express: Encouraging and Celebrating Great Performances
Gail Wasserman, American Express Corporation, New York, NY

Federal Express: Where Customers Absolutely, Positively Come First
Darlene Faquin, Federal Express, Memphis, TN